FAITH
That Pleases
GOD

BOB GEORGE

HARVEST HOUSE PUBLISHERS
Eugene, Oregon 97402

Cover by Koechel Peterson & Associates, Minneapolis, Minnesota

FAITH THAT PLEASES GOD
Copyright © 2001 by Bob George
Published by Harvest House Publishers
Eugene, Oregon 97402

Library of Congress Cataloging-in-Publication Data
George, Bob, 1933-
  Faith that pleases God / Bob George.
    p. cm.
  ISBN 0-7369-0139-6
  1. Faith. 2. George, Bob, 1933- I. Title.

BV4637 .G45 2001
234'.23—dc21   00-047128

Printed in the United States of America

01 02 03 04 05 06 07 08 09 10 / BP-MS / 10 9 8 7 6 5 4 3 2 1

Contents

A Message from Bob 5

1. My Introduction to Faith 9

2. Shifting Faith 25

3. Faith Must Have an Object 37

4. Faith: Initiator or Responder? 53

5. Responding to God's Offer of Life 65

6. Responding to the New Covenant 79

7. Hindrances to a Proper Response
   to Total Forgiveness 101

8. What the Bible Says About Confession
   and Forgiveness 121

9. Faith's Response to the Spirit's Leading 135

10. One Faith for All Men 159

11. Faith's Response to God's Offer of Rest 185

12. Faith Expressing Itself Through Love 201

Acknowledgments

I want to take this opportunity to thank my wife, Amy, for her dedication and help she gave me in producing this book. Amy has stood by my side for the last thirty years of ministry and has been through all of the experiences that have helped us to learn the grace of God. Her love and devotion is a true testimony of the work of the Holy Spirit in one's life.

My thanks goes to Nick Harrison of Harvest House Publishers, who took all of the concepts that God has revealed to me over the years and put them into written form.

Last but certainly not least least, I also want to thank my fellow worker Bob Christopher, who has been with me in the ministry for seventeen years. Bob's help has been invaluable to me in getting this manuscript developed, edited, and put into its final form. All of us devoted hundreds of hours to this project and in so doing learned more about faith that pleases God. It's my desire and prayer that the same will be true of you as you read and discern the meaning of Biblical faith.

A Message from Bob

FOR THE PAST 15 YEARS, OUR MINISTRY, People to People, has taken nearly 20,000 phone calls during our nationwide call-in radio program. During that time we've encountered just about every human problem imaginable. We've heard from the newly wed to the nearly dead. We've dealt with serious problems and frivolous problems. We've laughed with our callers, and we've also cried with them.

But in all those calls, I've noticed a pattern. Most of the Christian callers know what the Bible has to say, but they don't know how to respond in a way that will bring a solution to their situation. What they all seem to be asking is, "How does my Christian faith affect my _____?" And you can fill in the blank with words such as *depression, troubled marriage, anger, eating disorder, sexual addiction, drug or alcohol dependency,* or just about any other problem under the sun. In short, the callers want to know how their Christian faith can change their behavior.

As a result of these calls and the many counseling sessions we conduct at People to People, God has been focusing my attention on what faith is—and what it isn't. What's interesting is that everyone has faith. For example, a man who won't walk under a ladder has faith in superstition. The evolutionist has faith that random chance has resulted in human life. Anyone who goes to bed at night expecting to wake up in the morning has faith, even if the faith is simply that the world will still be turning on its axis the next morning.

Even atheists have faith. If you look at the life of the late Madalyn Murray O'Hair, the renowned atheist, you find that she exercised great *faith* that God doesn't exist. Religious people, of course, have faith. Faith is an important element of every religious system.

No, lack of faith isn't the real problem for most people. Nor is the amount of faith important. Jesus told His followers that anyone who simply had the faith of a small mustard seed could move a mountain. So if it isn't the absence of faith nor the amount of faith that matters, just what is it about faith that really counts in God's eyes? *What is the faith that pleases God?* The answer to that question is the most important truth a Christian can ever realize, and it's the reason for this book.

More than ten years ago, my first book, *Classic Christianity*, was published by Harvest House Publishers. In that book I mentioned my early experience as a Christian and the frustration I faced as I tried to live up to the expectations of those whose approval mattered most to me. My enjoyment of Christ was replaced by a treadmill of religious activity that left me as dry as the Mojave Desert on an August afternoon.

As I later discovered, my experience was typical of most Christians. *Classic Christianity* has now sold more than half a million copies worldwide, and I frequently receive letters and phone calls on our radio broadcast from readers who identify with my journey.

The popularity of *Classic Christianity* has also shown me that people are hungry for biblical truth that will change their lives. And the most profound, critical, and life-changing truth I've found is the truth about the kind of faith that pleases God. With this kind of faith we step off the treadmill and are once again able to enjoy our relationship with Christ Jesus.

Frankly, I'm convinced beyond all doubt that most Christians' troubles are inevitably a result of misunderstanding what true faith is, as seen through God's eyes. Instead, people are operating under a false faith that constantly needs bolstering. Vainly they try to muster up the kind of faith they think will please God and thus reverse their sad circumstances, little realizing that this, too, is a treadmill religion that in no way pleases God.

On the following pages I want to share the story of my early years as a believer and how I allowed my once-vibrant faith to be undermined. I have a hunch that what happened to me may sound very familiar to many of you, because you, too, have probably been down the same dusty road. You may, in fact, be camped out there right now. Of course, the details of your situation may be a bit different, but my guess is that the results are pretty much the same: You've lost sight of the gospel of grace and, like the first-century Galatian Christians, returned to what the apostle Paul called a "yoke of slavery."

If so, cheer up! Paul wrote to the Galatians to turn their faith around and get it pointed in the right direction. Down through the centuries many believers have faced those same struggles. And for every one of them, the answer was the same: Restoration is in learning to have the kind of faith that pleases God.

And it's not as hard as you think!

My Introduction to Faith

IN THE SMALL INDIANA FARMING community where I was raised, most everyone went to church. After all, it was the right thing to do. My dad was a respected lawyer, and so our family attended a nice, proper denominational church. Every Sunday we sat quietly in our pews listening to the pastor preach his sermon. What he said I couldn't tell you to save my life. As a young boy, all I wanted was for the sermon to end so I could play outside.

But there was one thing that happened in church that greatly interested me. Every Sunday the ushers passed little cups of grape juice up and down the pews, right under my eager nose. I watched that tray go past me and wondered why I couldn't have some. I *loved* grape juice, and so one day I asked my mother, "What do I have to do to be able to drink grape juice every Sunday like you and Dad?" She answered, "Bobby, you need to be baptized, then you can have communion."

"Well, lead me to the water!" I replied. If being immersed in some water granted me that privilege, I was all for it. So they baptized me in the name of the Father, the Son, and the Holy Ghost, and thereafter I was entitled to drink grape juice every Sunday morning. I didn't have a clue as to the ritual's meaning, but I sure enjoyed that grape juice. That was all I cared about.

A New Motivation

Not long after this, one of my school buddies, Tom Dailey, invited me to come to his church. This was an easy decision for me to make because in the basement they had a basketball court. The ceiling was only about eight feet high, but it was a *basketball court*—and in Indiana, basketball is king.

So now I found a religious motivation even greater than drinking grape juice—playing basketball. But in order to play ball, I had to join the church's youth choir. So just as I was baptized so that I could drink grape juice, I joined the choir to have a place to play basketball. Sunday after Sunday we all warbled like birds (except for Tom—he was tone-deaf), all the while itching for the service to be over so we could go down to the basement and play ball.

The pastor, Reverend Spurgeon, had a way of drawing youth to his church. He attracted kids like sugar attracts flies. Reverend Spurgeon loved us and we loved him. He involved us in all sorts of fun activities. He even bought a bus—something unheard of back then—to take us on field trips to New Castle's Memorial Park, where we would play baseball, football, and have all sorts of great fun. This pastor and his church were so popular that one Palm Sunday, in this tiny Indiana town, 300 of us young people came down the aisle waving palm branches and singing at the top of our lungs "Wonderful Grace of Jesus."

Everyone thought Reverend Spurgeon was great. He took me from my previous years of sitting in a dark church basement with maps of Israel all over the wall to a church experience that was actually fun for a young boy. There was just one problem: Reverend Spurgeon didn't know how to communicate the gospel to his captive audience. Perhaps he didn't know himself how to be saved. Sometimes he talked about Jesus, but never as a Savior whom we must trust for salvation. I never heard the words *lost, saved,* or *born again*.

I was having a lot of fun enjoying church activities and playing basketball with my buddies, but I didn't know what faith in Christ was all about.

Although basketball was my passion, I also had a talent for singing, so during my junior year of high school I entered a statewide singing contest. I was a baritone, and the song I sang was "Sweet Little Jesus Boy." It's a beautiful song, but for me the words packed a great deal of irony. The song concludes with the admission, "We didn't know who You was."

I was singing my own testimony. I really *didn't* know who Jesus was. I knew *about* Jesus. I believed He was the Son of God and that He died on a cross. I even believed that He was raised from the dead. But I didn't know that He died for *me*. I didn't even know that I was a sinner in need of a Savior, much less that Jesus *was* that Savior.

I remember many times during the Christmas season lying on the floor in our living room in front of our radio listening to Christmas carols, so moved by the words that tears streamed down my cheeks. I honestly believe that had anyone come to me as a young boy and told me about the need to accept Jesus as my Savior, I would have done so without hesitation.

As it was, the words of those carols and the hymns we sang in church on Sunday, along with many of my early childhood religious experiences, softened my heart for a future day when I would finally understand. Many people have told me that they, too, can look back at their youth and recall experiences where they felt an openness and love for God, even though they didn't know what it was they actually were supposed to believe about Him.

As for the singing competition, I did win first prize, but I still didn't know who Jesus was.

Defending the Faith

In the summer following my senior year of high school, my mother and I headed for New York City where I would audition for the popular television program *Arthur Godfrey's Talent Scouts*. Winning the competition on Arthur Godfrey's program was a ticket to success as a performer. Older readers will remember Julius LaRosa, Pat Boone, the McGuire Sisters, Jimmie Rodgers—these were just a few who started their careers with a win on this prestigious program. I wanted to follow in their footsteps.

Upon my arrival in New York, I was introduced to Mrs. Elizabeth Stoll and Mr. Larry Puck, who were in charge of the auditions. Coming from Indiana, I found New York intimidating enough, but being in the presence of those who could literally affect me for the rest of my life was overwhelming. After three auditions, I was notified that I had won the opportunity for my once-in-a-lifetime chance to compete on the *Arthur Godfrey* show!

The next day I was introduced to the vice president of Columbia Records, Arthur Willi. Mr. Willi was a very gentle man and one whose honesty changed the direction of my life. He informed me that they were ready to offer me a contract, but there was something I should consider first. He told me that he held a job that would be the envy of 99 percent of the people in the world, but that he had one regret. He had never finished college. He advised me that if I signed with Columbia Records, they would in essence own me, and there would never be a chance for me to even begin, let alone finish, my college education. When he finished speaking, I knew I had a choice to make.

My dad had always taught me that there's one thing no one can ever take away from me, and that's what is in my head. Getting an education was always paramount in his and my mind. At Mr. Willi's suggestion I took a day to think about what he said before deciding what to do. This was one tremendously big decision for an 18-year-old. That night I spotted a large church in the middle of New York City. I didn't know or care that it was a Catholic church; all I wanted was a place to go to talk with God. After about an hour the decision was made: I was going to get my education! Mr. Willi assured me that the contract would be waiting for me upon graduation.

That fall, I started my college training at DePauw University in Greencastle, Indiana. The following year I transferred to Indiana University, where I once again joined my buddies Tom Dailey (the tone-deaf one),

Johnny Black, Jerry Ellis, and the rest of the gang from New Castle.

College was fun, but my church activities ceased. Of course I attended church on Easter and Christmas, and I certainly still believed in Jesus. I was never anti-Jesus or even skeptical about Him, but I just didn't see any reason to go to church every Sunday. After all, by now I no longer craved the taste of grape juice, and the church I attended near the college didn't have a basketball court in the basement, so why bother?

But one day while still in college I had an experience that exposed the shallow faith I had thought of as real. One of my fraternity brothers made a disparaging remark about Christ. I don't remember exactly what he said, but it was enough to cause me to punch him in the nose. That was my idea of "defending the faith"—pulverize the guys who don't believe in Jesus!

Success at Home and in Business

After graduation I still had the mandatory draft of the army waiting for me, so once again Columbia Records was put on hold. In order to "hedge my bet" in the event that the entertainment business wasn't what it was cracked up to be, I interviewed and was accepted into the training program of the Armstrong Company out of Lancaster, Pennsylvania. When my six-month floor-covering training with Armstrong was complete, I began my two-year stretch in the army. I was assigned to Germany, where I had the tough duty of going into special services and putting on shows for soldiers. This was my first exposure to being in the entertainment business full-time.

During my first week in Germany I met the girl who would become my wife. I hadn't been looking for a wife and wasn't much interested in marriage, but when I saw Amy, I knew she was the one. Within a year she became Mrs. Bob George.

During those two years in the army, something happened in the entertainment business. Rock 'n' roll had emerged with Elvis as the king! When my military service was completed, I returned to America and immediately called Mr. Willi. His comment to me was, "Bob, I'm sorry, but Sinatra isn't making it today. There is no way for you to make it, either." You would think that news would have devastated me, but quite frankly it didn't. I had two years of full-time entertainment in the service and realized that, sure enough, it wasn't what I thought it would be. With this news I merely turned my attention back to my career with Armstrong. They assigned me first to Dallas, then San Antonio, then Kansas City. During these years our two children were born, and my company promoted me regularly every 18 months.

These promotions weren't quite fast enough for me, so in an effort to speed things up in my career, I took a new job in the Los Angeles area and was soon making more money than I could spend, driving a beautiful black Lincoln Continental convertible, and hobnobbing with movie stars. In fact, I refer to those years as the years of cars, bars, and movie stars.

Eventually I had the opportunity to own a floor-covering distributorship in the Los Angeles area and worked hard to make it succeed. And I wasn't disappointed. My business grew, and Amy and I prospered. We had a nice home with a swimming pool. We had lots of friends, went to many fun parties, and had plenty of money in the bank. But on the inside I was empty and spiritually bankrupt, though no one knew it by looking at me from the outside.

In those days, when I met with a customer to do business, the bar was the most logical place to meet—and I met with a lot of customers. In fact, I never knew there were coffee shops to meet in till after I got saved.

As I look back on those years, I've often asked myself, "Why did I go to all those bars?" It wasn't just to meet customers. It wasn't to drink—I really didn't care for the taste of alcohol that much. The truth is, during those empty years I had an insatiable desire for acceptance from people. So I became a regular at the bars where I could have "fellowship" with my buddies. We would drink and tell off-color jokes hour after hour. All the while I would be reveling in the acceptance I received, especially when they laughed at my funny stories.

After many nights of my arriving home late, Amy strangely didn't think my jokes were very funny, nor did she care for my drinking and staying out with the guys. With a lack of acceptance and a critical attitude waiting for me at home, you can guess where I preferred to be. It was with the guys at the bar who I thought accepted me and my crude humor along with the drinking. And, of course, all this was done under the auspices of "business."

And it was true, my business was booming—a sure sign of success to everyone out there. In fact, I was so engrossed with my business and my success that when my parents flew to Los Angeles for a visit, I didn't take them directly home first, but to my warehouse to show them how I had really made it in this world.

As I expanded the business and grew financially, I grew even poorer inside. I began to ask myself what was wrong with me. I had everything that the world said would make me happy, and yet I was miserable—bigtime miserable.

At about this same time, I attended a Billy Graham crusade in Los Angeles. As the great evangelist preached, I felt like he was talking right to me, even though we sat far away. At the end of his message Billy Graham issued the traditional invitation for people to come forward, to repent of sins, and to accept Christ as Lord and Savior. The phrase "repent of sins" stopped me dead in my tracks. What I was hearing was that Christianity wasn't trusting in Christ, but trusting in my ability to do better—to quit sinning and give up the old lifestyle and the things I enjoyed. I had broken enough New Year's resolutions to know I couldn't change myself, so I didn't go forward. My heart was open, but my misunderstanding of what I thought the gospel was kept me from responding to Christ.

After the crusade, I went home and continued my life as before. Except now I decided that what I truly needed to do was grow even richer, so I opened a branch of my business in San Diego. But that didn't work. I was still empty inside. I was also becoming keenly aware of my inability to love. In an attempt to be honest with Amy, I admitted to her that I loved her as much as I could, but that it wasn't very much. Sadly, I looked at other fathers I knew, and they seemed to have a deep love for their children that I wasn't experiencing.

Every morning as I looked at myself in the mirror I asked, "Why can't I be the kind of husband and father and man I know I should be? Why am I doing so well in business, but am such a failure as a person?"

I was especially down on myself when I compared myself to Dad. He was a good husband and father and one of the most moral men I had ever known. His word meant everything. And it was through my dad that God finally got my attention.

My Bargain with God

One day I got a call from Mom telling me that Dad had been diagnosed with throat cancer. In fact, he had just returned from the hospital, where he had a portion of his throat removed.

I'll never forget flying back to my parents' home to visit them during this hard time. My dad looked tired, worn down, and pitiful. He had lost so much weight. He was down to only 110 pounds. He told me in a garbled voice, "Bob, I've worked all my life to have enough money to eat anything that I wanted to eat, and now I've got the money but I can't eat."

And it was true. My dad could no longer eat. Even water wouldn't stay down. My heart sank as I watched my dad suffer.

That night when Mom and Dad had gone to bed, I broke down and cried like a baby. I hadn't cried in years, but that night the dam broke loose. I had been told early in my career that nice guys finish last and that I was a nice guy. I had gotten the message that I needed to toughen up if I wanted to succeed. As a result, my heart had become as hard as a brick over the years. However, seeing my dad that night cracked the surface. I found myself praying the words of a song that was popular then—"What's it all about, Alfie?"—as I searched for answers.

There had to be something more to life than working and making money, day after day. But I didn't know what it was. "God," I prayed, "if there's any meaning to this life, You're going to have to show me what it is, because I can't figure it out."

During the next several months I flew back and forth to be with Mom and Dad. On one of these trips, we got the news that the cancer had spread to Dad's stomach and was causing a bowel obstruction. He had grown so weak that I knew he probably couldn't survive the surgery the doctor said was necessary. In utter desperation, I found myself in the hospital chapel on my knees, begging, praying, and promising, "God, if You get my dad well, I'll dedicate my life to You."

Naturally, I assumed that God couldn't pass up a deal like this. Hey, this was *Bob George, successful businessman,* offering God a great deal. How could He resist?

And sure enough, when the day of surgery arrived, the mass had mysteriously disappeared from Dad's stomach. He was up and had shaved himself—something he hadn't been able to do for some time because of his weakened condition. My mom said, "You know, there was a minister who's been coming by to visit with us. I bet he had something to do with this."

"Mom," I said, "I think you're right."

Under my breath I said, "Thank You, God," as I also determined to go right back to my old lifestyle. The deal with God was off as far as I was concerned. God had done His part, but now that Dad was going to be well, I saw my responsibility to God in a different light.

But God was at work. During the following months strange things began to happen. For one thing, as Dad's health continued to improve, I got worse. I remember one night after spending several hours with some friends in a bar, I came home and lied to Amy about where I'd been. As a result, we got into a big fight. When things simmered down, we stepped outside for a walk.

After a few minutes of silence, hesitatingly I said, "You know, honey, there is such a tugging at my heart that sometimes I think God wants me to be a minister or something." To my surprise, Amy responded, "Well, why don't you go to school and learn to be one?"

I didn't understand that God wasn't calling me to be a minister; He was calling me to Himself. So often we think that He wants us to do something, like full-time Christian work, when in reality all God wants us to do is come to Him.

The only true calling anyone ever really gets is "Come unto Me." From that one specific calling, the result might be that He'll then send us somewhere. But the real calling of God is to *Him*, not to something or somewhere.

The Good News of the Gospel

As Amy and I returned from our walk, we sat down in our living room to watch TV. As I was scanning through the channels, we came across a program hosted by Campus Crusade for Christ, starring Pat Boone. During the program, Pat introduced some sharp-looking young people who were athletes. They said that they had found "power for living" in the Person of Jesus Christ. I will never forget the words of the Olympic gold medalist weight lifter, Russ Knipp, who said, "All my life I have searched for power, and I found it in the Person of Jesus Christ."

I had not heard that before, but my heart was touched. At the end of the program, a book was offered to anyone who would write in, which we did. Several weeks later we received a note that the book was back-ordered. However, they sent an invitation to an open house at Arrowhead Springs, California, in the San Bernardino Mountains.

At first I eagerly accepted the invitation, but then as the day approached, my enthusiasm faded and I tried to figure a way to get out of going.

Unable to find a good excuse, I reluctantly drove to Arrowhead Springs, where Amy and I sat in the back row of a huge outdoor auditorium as Bill Bright, president of Campus Crusade for Christ, spoke about Jesus. He wasn't talking about church. Not about being good. Not about religion. But about Jesus.

When he finished, I told Amy, "I've got to talk to that man." I told Dr. Bright about all my confusion and emptiness. After listening, he simply asked me, "Bob, have you ever made the wonderful discovery of knowing Christ personally?" I didn't know nor really understand what he was talking about, but as he continued to share the gospel with me, he finally asked if I would like to pray with him right then to receive Christ Jesus into my life.

Convicted by the Word of God and amid a flood of tears, I agreed with an open heart. Dr. Bright prayed with me, and in a simple, childlike manner, I responded to God's offer of new life in Christ Jesus. I finally understood the invitation Billy Graham had given at his crusade. It was to accept *Christ*. I was receiving the *gift* of a new life. It was not my making a commitment to try and do better in the future. Dr. Bright made this plain as he shared the words of Ephesians 2:8,9 with me: "For it is by grace you have been saved, through faith—and this not from yourselves, it is the gift of God—not by works, so that no one can boast."

Within a few moments, Dr. Bright had also talked and prayed with Amy, who solidified her surrender to the Lord that day.

A miracle? Yes, it was certainly a miracle. God took a man with an empty heart and He filled it with Himself. He took a marriage headed for the divorce courts and restored it. From that day on, Amy and I have served the Lord together for the past 33 years.

You could combine all the "miracles" you see on television. You could cut my leg off and see it grow back, and it still wouldn't compare to what happened to me that day. I experienced the greatest miracle anyone could ever witness. I found the deepest need of my heart satisfied by the Lord Jesus Christ.

After we arrived home from Arrowhead Springs, I began in earnest to tell everyone about Jesus. And, like most eager and zealous new believers, the first people I wanted to share with were members of my family. I knew that my mom and dad were in the same condition I had been all my life: religious, yet lost. They knew about Jesus, but they didn't know Him personally.

I was so concerned that my parents hear the gospel communicated correctly that I flew back to Indiana, picked them up, and flew them back to California so that Dr. Bright could talk to Dad and tell him what he told me. I figured he did such a good job with me, he couldn't miss with my dad, who, I knew, had just a few months left to live.

When Dr. Bright shared with Dad and asked if he would like to receive Christ, Dad said, "Dr. Bright, I would be happy to pray with you, but you have to understand that I've lived a very moral life. In our church we have quite an array of stained glass windows. Dr. Bright, I paid for those windows—every one of them." My heart sank as I listened to the conversation. My mind raced with concern at the thought that my dad was lost and dying.

We went home and, in another attempt to reach my dad, I gave him a book to read. I was so anxious for my dad to receive Christ that sometimes I felt like I was badgering him. I also realized how seriously ill he was, and I didn't want to upset him. But this was important. I couldn't watch my dad die without knowing Christ.

When my parents returned to Indiana, Dad's health took a turn for the worse. All of my family assembled to be with him for what we knew was our last opportunity to see Dad, and I wanted desperately to know for sure that he had eternal life.

In my heart, I cried out to God: "I've got to know about Dad's relationship with You. Please, God, don't let him die without knowing You." As our visit over the long weekend finally drew to a close, Dad summoned my brother and me into his hospital room.

Fragile, thin, and gaunt, he looked at us and said, "Boys, I want you to know that all the things I placed so much importance on during my life are meaningless. The only thing that really matters is man and his relationship with God." Then Dad turned to me and said, "Bob, I read that book you gave me, and everything's A-OK."

I leaned over and kissed my dad a final kiss. That day I left to go back to California, and by the time I arrived home from the airport, the telephone was ringing with the news that my father had died. My reaction was simply, "Thank You, Lord. Thank You for giving me a wonderful father. Thank You for saving me and for allowing me to be a vehicle for You to save Dad. I know where I am going one day, and now I know for sure where Dad is: 'absent from the body and present with the Lord.' "

It wasn't long after that when my mom also came to know Jesus. Then my brother, Dick, who had battled alcohol for many years, received Christ and was freed of alcohol dependency that day. He has walked with the Lord for the past 30 years. After that, my sister, Eileen, also received Jesus into her heart. My whole family was eventually brought to Christ.

Seeing in real life what God can do, I finally understood that Christianity isn't about me and my ability to change my life. It is about *Christ* and *His* ability to change me. All I had to do was respond by faith.

Shifting 2 Faith

As a result of my surrender to Christ, my priorities in life changed. Everything was different now. Second Corinthians 5:17 says, "Therefore, if anyone is in Christ, he is a new creation; the old has gone, the new has come!" That was certainly true of me. There was a freshness of spirit as I entered what could be called the honeymoon phase of my new life in Christ.

As for my business, I had a new attitude toward success. If a salesman brought in a $20,000 order, I would say, "That's nice. Now let me tell you about Jesus." Obviously, that is *not* the way to encourage a salesman to sell more.

During this period of our lives, Amy and I attended a small denominational church pastored by a liberal minister whose sermons never mentioned the gospel message. I was so excited about sharing my newfound faith with everyone that I approached the pastor and asked if I could teach a Bible study. He agreed, and I started the following Sunday. This pastor was so liberal in his views that had I asked him if I could teach a class on how to bark at the moon, he would probably have agreed to that, also.

Brand new to the Bible myself, I started the study by going through the same message that I had responded to by inviting Christ into my life. That first Sunday, 18 of the 21 people attending indicated that they came to know Christ. That small church quickly ignited into new life and became one of the strongest evangelistic churches of its denomination in that community.

It certainly wasn't through my efforts. This was God's work. I was just responding to what God had done in my life and acting on my desire to share this good news with others.

This spiritual honeymoon continued to the point where one day I found myself kneeling beside my desk, praying, "God, put me where You want me. If You want me to remain as a businessman, I'll happily stay. If You want me in full-time Christian work, work out the details."

Amy, however, had a slightly different attitude. She had been brought up in abject poverty, and she thought that full-time Christian work meant a return to the poverty of her youth. If that was the case, she wanted no part of it.

During the next two years I waited for Amy's heart to change. Then one day after she attended a Bible study on the life of Abraham, Amy said, "I don't want to miss God's blessing. I'm ready."

That was my cue. I sold my business, and we began a life of trusting Christ for our needs. That was 30 years ago, and we've never looked back with regret.

So two years after becoming a Christian I entered full-time Christian work with Campus Crusade for Christ. I went from being a highly ambitious, successful entrepreneur to being a Christian worker who had to raise his own support of $540 a month. It was quite a change in lifestyle.

Full-time ministry was exciting for me. I couldn't believe my daily job was to be part of a team proclaiming the good news of Jesus Christ. This is what I had longed for since the day I received Christ. Everything was going great for me—at least for a while. But soon that old desire for acceptance raised its ugly head and started creeping back into my life. I began to notice the accolades some of my fellow staff members were receiving: the pats on the back, the strokes, the commendations. I started to ask myself, "What do I have to do to get some of that attention?"

It wasn't long before I figured out that my successful evangelistic activity brought applause from the people whose opinion I valued the most.

Being involved in leading many people to the Savior is what led me into full-time Christian service. But now, rather than sharing the gospel because I wanted others to know Christ, I was witnessing to people and anticipating the praise and acceptance that was ahead for me. With my sales background and training, evangelism wasn't that hard. Instead of selling floor coverings, I was selling Jesus. As embarrassing as it is to admit, I remember sharing Christ and looking out of the corner of my eye to see if anyone was watching.

Sure enough, I started getting those strokes I desired, and I truly felt accepted by my peers. The leadership even considered me "spiritually mature." That label earned me more respect and more responsibility.

Busy but Barren

Within two years I was sent to Dallas to pioneer Campus Crusade's "Here's Life" project, which along with Atlanta was to be the template for their national "I Found It" campaign. So off we moved to Dallas, where I had a large staff under my direction. We trained thousands of lay workers, enlisted churches to help, handled advertising, logistics, phone banks—everything. It was a huge undertaking. I nearly worked myself to death.

Amy and I began to attend one of the largest churches in Dallas, where I could use the facilities to help train people. Before long the pastor heard about this excited young man, a new member of his church, who was eager to evangelize, and he asked me if I could also serve as evangelism director of his congregation. Of course, I said yes, and so now I had two jobs.

Then after a while, the church bought a radio station, and I was asked if I would do a daily 15-minute program. Again, I said yes. Now I had three jobs. Next, I was asked to teach evangelism and discipleship at the local Bible college. I said yes, and now I had four jobs.

Here I was, with a sincere heart, wanting to please the Lord. But really what I was looking for—again—was acceptance from people. I found myself on this treadmill of Christian activity, going at the speed of a hamster. I wasn't going anyplace, but I was making good time. Loaded down with evangelism, Bible memorization, witnessing, visitation, prayer meetings, church attendance, and radio broadcasts, my faith shifted from listening and responding to the love of Christ to totally seeking the approval of men.

This subtle shift from faith to works was similar to the one for which Paul had rebuked the Galatian church. The apostle had posed the question to the Galatians, "Am I now trying to win the approval of men, or of God? Or am I trying to please men? If I were still trying to please men, I would not be a servant of Christ" (Galatians 1:10). The "foolish" Galatians, as Paul called them, had begun well by accepting Christ by faith. But they were trying to advance in the Christian life through legalism. Having begun in grace, they had now "fallen from grace" by trying to keep the law of acceptance through works.

Paul even had some harsh words for Peter in this regard. In chapter 2 he recalls how Peter once ate and fellowshipped with the Gentiles, but then "began to draw back and separate himself from the Gentiles because he was afraid of those who belonged to the circumcision group" (Galatians 2:12). The result of Peter's attempts to please men rather than God was that "the other Jews joined him in his hypocrisy, so that by their hypocrisy, even Barnabas was led astray" (verse 13).

Like the Galatians and like Peter, I was no longer responding to the grace of God. Instead, I was motivated by my desire for acceptance, and the acceptance I sought came through performance.

Something was wrong, and I finally saw what it was. My emphasis had become *activity* for Jesus, not *communion* with Jesus. And yet I had been told that if I prayed, witnessed, studied my Bible, and got involved, I would be happy. And here I was doing all those things in excess and yet crying in misery on my way to work each morning. I had totally lost the joy of my salvation. I was miserable and had embarked on that journey common to many believers wherein the excitement of knowing Christ begins to wane, only to be replaced by endless attempts to be pleasing to God and those whose opinion matters. Man, not God, had became the object of my faith. I had discovered the surefire formula to burnout for Jesus.

In the myriad of activity I cried out one morning, "Lord, I'm miserable. You know it and I know it. I'm sincere—but, God, I'm *exhausted*. According to Your Word I should be experiencing freedom. But, God, I'm the most trapped person I know."

Then through the dry bones of my spirit, it was as if God was saying, "Bob, I didn't say keeping busy would set you free, nor did I say that reading My Word would set you free. Or witnessing. Or teaching. Or radio broadcasts. I said the truth would set you free. *I am that truth.* And when the Son has set you free, you shall be free indeed [John 8:36]."

I began to see how my faith had shifted over the short lapse of time since I had accepted Christ. I had subtly shifted my faith from truth to error. And now I saw that if truth sets you free, then error puts you in bondage. It isn't complicated. The reason we get messed up is that we substitute error for truth.

I told God, "If I am caught up in error, then I want to know truth." I asked God to push all error out of my mind and replace it with His truth. And God began to reason with me. "Bob, your mind is like a blackboard covered with all sorts of religious information. You have some good info on it and some bad. When you're trying to sort out the good from the bad, you get confused. Bob, today let's erase the whole thing and start over. I don't care what the Baptists or what Campus Crusade has taught you, or your pastor, relative, or friend. I want you to erase it all and start over again, allowing Me to teach you. Are you willing?"

I answered, "Lord, am I ever!"

"Good," God said. "Now, open your Bible."

As I did, over the course of the next several months, God began to teach me the fullness of His grace—starting with the very basics.

Supplement or Substitute?

One of the first things I learned was that what God blesses as a supplement to our faith, He will later curse as a substitute. The Sunday school class you teach to supplement your faith can soon become a substitute. The daily regimen of a quiet time can even shift from a supplement to your faith to a hollow substitute. That's what happened to me. My "works" for Him, by which I was supplementing my faith, mutated into an empty substitute for a joyous faith in His completed work.

Another reason that our faith can shift so readily from resting in God's approval to trying to gain His acceptance is that we tend to see our relationship with God in the same way we view our relationship with our earthly father.

While most children never question a mother's love, they have an insatiable desire for their dad's approval and acceptance. A daughter looks for love from her dad. Sons want to know that their father accepts them. Many never experience that acceptance, and so they search all their lives to satisfy the spiritual hunger that only God can fill. I know grown men and women in their thirties and forties and beyond who are still trying to gain the recognition and acceptance of a human father.

That's how I was. Remember when my parents came to visit me in Los Angeles and I took them by my new warehouse instead of directly to my home? It wasn't for my mother's sake as much as my father's. I wanted my dad to see and approve of my success.

That same motive sneaks into our relationship with God. We want that same kind of approval from God. As a result, we take God on tours of our spiritual successes. Maybe not as brashly, but just as certainly. We lead several people to Christ, and they become like gold statues in our spiritual trophy case. Or we teach Sunday school year after year. Or we serve on the deacon board, or—as my father did—we buy stained glass windows for the church. We want something to show to our Father to prove our worthiness to Him. Our faith has shifted and we soon feel the dismal results.

But when we learn to rest by faith in our heavenly Father's acceptance and total approval of us in Christ, we'll be free from the struggle for our earthly father's approval. We will be free indeed.

I had come to the Lord as a very self-sufficient lost man, and I became a very self-sufficient saved man. That self-dependence, or independence from God for many of us, carries over into our Christian life. We think, "Boy, God can sure use my talents." That statement is a clear indication of someone whose faith has shifted from Christ to self.

Have you ever thought, "If only that athlete or that actress or that politician became a Christian, wow, what a witness they could be for Christ"?

If so, your thinking is natural, fleshly, man-oriented. You're leaning on your own understanding, not God's. Consider the men Jesus picked as His disciples. Although there were athletes, celebrities, and politicians in His day, He chose primarily simple fishermen and tax collectors who were unimportant to man, but who had a heart for God.

Fleshly thinking, particularly that which I call the "religious flesh," is a sure sign of shifted faith. This is nothing more than looking at people and things from a human perspective. And until we have our minds renewed with truth and start depending on Christ to allow us to see everything and everyone through His eyes, we'll never change. But thanks be to God, He doesn't leave us in our ignorance. When we ask Him to be our eyes and to let us think His thoughts, His grace will push out the error and replace it with truth. You see, God doesn't need our ability, only our availability.

Legalism and Works

The two primary errors to which we shift our faith are legalism and works. The former is trying to please God by living according to stringent laws, principles, and regulations. The latter is trying to please God through our own good works. Although I wasn't bogged down in legalism, I had shifted my faith to works. Either error kills spiritual life because both originate from "self" and not from Christ.

We can be controlled by self with its error, or we can be controlled by the truth of Christ. We can't be controlled by both.

Picture yourself in one of those old driver-education cars. If you remember, these cars had two steering wheels, two gas pedals, two brakes, and so forth. Pretend you're in one seat, and the Lord is in the other. He says to you, "My child, I have great plans for you. I will reveal Myself to you, shower you with My love and acceptance, set you free by renewing your mind with My truth, and conform you to My image as we go through life together. All you have to do is enjoy the ride and let Me drive. But notice that in front of you is your own set of driving controls. You have the capability and freedom of grabbing the steering wheel and taking things into your own hands. Only one of us can drive at a time, and the choice is yours. If you take control, I will take My hands off. I promise that, whatever you choose, I will never leave you nor forsake you. But isn't it far better to allow Me to drive? I love you. I have all wisdom, all power, and I am committed to your ultimate good. I ask you to trust Me, but you are always free to choose. I died to set you free—not to make you a slave to sin, but so you can be My friend."

Under the influence of error, fear, or unbelief, we're often tempted to grab the wheel and drive ourselves. We even think at times that if we give Christ total control that He will cause something bad to happen to us to test us. The enemy is constantly trying to put thoughts like this into our mind to keep our hands on the wheel and so fool us into thinking that we are in control. The Lord, however, can be depended on because He continues to be faithful.

Also, people sometimes erroneously assume that if they give Christ total control, they'll simply be passive and won't be doing anything for God. However, if Jesus is alive and living in you, He will give you the desire to do His will. Just like the car that Jesus is driving moves in a certain direction, so will the Christian who is controlled by Jesus move forward in fruitful living.

We each have a life to live unto God wherein He, in control of our life, can produce the works He's planned for us. "For we are God's workmanship, created in Christ Jesus to do good works, which God prepared in advance for us to do" (Ephesians 2:10).

When I came to the end of my religious activity for the Lord, I was able to begin the real work God had for me. And, thank God, He's enabled me to do it ever since. The ministry of People to People began as God initiated it step-by-step. The result has been books, seminars, radio broadcasts, counseling, and all that goes into this ministry. I'm a busy man—perhaps as busy as when I was living in self-effort and bondage. But now there's a big difference. Before, the work was dry and draining. Now I don't look at it as work, but pure joy. And that's because I'm not doing the work, but Jesus is doing it through me by giving me His desire first.

There's been another important change in my work since I came to understand salvation. Before, when I was so busy working for God, I was always concerned about the results. After all, it was the results that brought me the applause I sought. But when I learned to rest in Christ, I was able to leave all the results to Him. And interestingly, the results of my ministry today are more fruitful than when I labored so hard pursuing results.

Remember, results are *always* God's business.

What happens when you share Christ with another person? You leave the results to God. I've never converted a single person. God does that. I don't take credit when someone prays to receive Christ, but I also don't beat myself up if he or she doesn't.

You can make and execute plans, but the results are up to God. I can write a book like this, but the results are in God's hands. Whatever it is that God calls you to do, don't examine your success by what your eye can see. Leave the results to God. That is the faith that pleases God.   ·

Faith Must Have an Object

ONE OF THE FIRST VERSES I learned as a new Christian was John 10:10 (NASB): "I came that they might have life, and might have it abundantly." I knew that this promise from God was true because, after my conversion, my life *had* been abundant. I really did experience the joy common to most new Christians.

But after two years of full-time service, what had happened to this abundant life? Where had it gone? How did I lose it? More importantly, how could I get it back?

Over the course of the next months and even years, I began to see the errors I had believed and how easily I had fallen into the subtle traps that had robbed me of my joy.

Probably the most important thing I learned had to do with what faith is and what it isn't, and the important difference between faith and belief. In the original Greek of the New Testament, the words translated to our English words *faith* and *belief* have the same meaning. But in our understanding of these two words today, they convey different concepts.

Belief is when we assume certain things are true or will happen, without having it make much difference in our lives. For instance, we can believe it will rain tomorrow or that the Democrats or Republicans will win the elections or that the Dallas Cowboys will win the Superbowl.

In Christianity, we can believe the doctrines of the faith but still not have faith. As a child, I knew Jesus was the Son of God, but I didn't have a clue as to what that meant. And how can you respond in faith if you don't know what something means? Oh, I said I had faith, but it had no value or substance whatsoever. *The kind of faith that pleases God is faith in what the Word of God means, not merely in what it says.*

James clearly tells us that even demons believe in Christ—and they tremble (James 2:19). They *believe* in Christ, as do many religious people. But they don't have the faith it takes to live in a trust relationship with Him.

Major Ian Thomas, author of the now-classic book *The Saving Life of Christ,* addressed this difference between belief and true faith in his foreword to my first book, *Classic Christianity.*

> There are few things quite so boring as being religious, but there is nothing quite so exciting as being a Christian.
>
> Most folks have never discovered the difference between the one and the other, so that there are those who sincerely try to live a life they do not have, substituting religion for God, Christianity for Christ, and their own noble endeavors for the energy, joy, and power of the Holy Spirit. In the absence of reality, they can only grasp at

ritual, stubbornly defending the latter in the absence of the former, lest they be found with neither!

They are lamps without oil, cars without gas, and pens without ink, baffled at their own impotence in the absence of all that alone can make man functional; for man was so engineered by God that the presence of the Creator within the creature is indispensable to His humanity. Christ gave Himself for us to give Himself to us! His presence puts God back into the man! He came that we might have life—God's life!

There are those who have a life they never live. They have come to Christ and thanked Him only for what He did, but do not live in the power of who He is. Between the Jesus who "was" and the Jesus who "will be" they live in a spiritual vacuum, trying with no little zeal to live for Christ a life that only He can live in and through them, perpetually begging for what in Him they already have.

I have always jokingly said that *Classic Christianity* is a commentary on Major Thomas's foreword. His description of those trying to live for God is a perfect picture of a person who may know what the Bible says, but who has never exercised faith in what it means.

Satan knows what the Bible says. He knows that Jesus is the Son of God. In fact, he could join any church in town.

If the pastor were to ask him, "Do you believe Jesus is the Son of God?"

"Yes," Satan would answer truthfully.

"Do you believe that Jesus died on the cross for the sins of the world?"

"Sure do. I was there."

"Do you believe He was raised from the dead?"

"Yes, I saw that, too."

"Do you believe He's now seated in the heavenlies at the right hand of the Father?"

"Sure. I zoom up there and try to talk to Him all the time."

Satisfied with these answers, the pastor would say, "Give him a tithing envelope. He's a member!"

Believing the historical facts presented in the Bible isn't salvation. To be saved involves changing that historical belief into personal faith that Jesus died for *my* sins and was raised from the dead to give *me* His life.

Many Christians are steadfast in reading their Bibles daily. Some can even recite large portions from memory. That may be good, but remember: Satan knows every word of the Bible. So it takes more than just reading or memorizing the words on the page.

For instance, I can be hungry and walk into a restaurant and ask the waiter for a menu. I can see that they serve a real nice sirloin steak, that their Caesar salad is prepared just the way I like it, and that their dessert bar is mouthwatering. But as long as I'm just reading the menu, what good is it doing for my starving stomach? You have to act on what you read, whether that means ordering food from the menu of your favorite restaurant or appropriating a promise from the Word of God.

Reading the Bible can plant a seed. Even belief in the doctrines of Christianity can be a seed that could sprout into faith. But then again, it may not. Belief may always be just that: a passive acknowledgment that something may happen or is true.

Faith, on the other hand, actively proves, appropriates, or accesses real truth. It's an action taken by man toward a promise that God has made. Faith internalizes what we say we believe.

Would You Get in the Wheelbarrow?

The best example of faith versus belief is well illustrated by the story of the tightrope walker crossing over Niagara Falls. For many years, until it was outlawed, Niagara Falls was a favorite place for tightrope walkers to show off their daring acts. It was, after all, an extremely dangerous stunt to walk across that great chasm with the water roaring beneath. Crowds loved to watch these daredevils and their antics. One of the men, Blondin, carried a woodstove on his back, and midway through the walk he stopped and cooked an omelette with the woodstove perched on the tightrope. Once he carried his manager across the expanse on his back.

But the best story of all involves the tightrope walker who walked his wheelbarrow across the tightrope to everyone's applause. Then he asked the crowd, "Do you think I could put a person in the wheelbarrow and push him across the great chasm?" Of course, the crowd cheered. They had seen similar stunts. They had watched as the Great Blondin had carried his manager across on his back.

After the cheering subsided, the great tightrope walker turned the wheelbarrow toward the crowd and asked, "Who will volunteer?"

There was a strange silence. Everyone *believed* the daredevil could do it. They had seen his performances before. It was certain to be successful. And, of course, someone from the crowd *should* volunteer. Everyone agreed on that point. But strangely, everyone thought someone other than himself should be the volunteer.

That true story illustrates the difference between belief and faith. They all believed, but no one was willing to step forward and transform that belief into practical faith.

Many "believers" truly believe that Christ can save them, just as the onlookers believed that the tightrope walker could take them in a wheelbarrow across Niagara Falls. But when it comes to demonstrating faith in the venture by getting into the wheelbarrow, or demonstrating faith by fully making Christ alone the object of their faith, many people balk.

When I understood the difference between faith and belief, I was able to see how my once newfound faith, full of joy and excitement, had shifted away from Jesus Christ to lesser objects, such as man's approval of my efforts and what people thought of me.

You see, faith *always* has an object. And the value of a person's faith is directly related to the value of the object of that faith. Faith that's focused solely on Christ as its object will bring happiness, security, and fruitfulness. Faith in anything less is misplaced and will lead to the fruit of error: frustration, stagnation, bondage, and struggle.

For example, someone may say, "Swallowing enables you to live," and that sounds reasonable at first. But you can also swallow and die, if what you swallow is poison. So it's not the act of swallowing that enables you to live, but swallowing *food* that enables you to live. You can swallow poison and die, using the identical mechanism that you use to swallow food to live! In the same way, faith doesn't save us. *Faith in the Lord Jesus Christ saves us!*

This kind of faith is directed to the One who claimed to be "the way and the truth and the life" (John 14:6). When Christ is the object of our faith, we also have *truth* as the object of our faith. The result is that truth sets us free and keeps us free from slavery and bondage to erroneous thinking and action. When our faith shifts away from the truth, guess to where it shifts? To error! And what does error do? It puts us in bondage.

As human beings, we're prone to such shifting with little provocation. It's our nature to lean on our own understanding. That's why we need a firm foundation, based in truth that's objective and outside of ourselves, on which to rely.

Christ as the Plumb Line

In terms a carpenter would understand, God has designated Christ for us as a "plumb line." When erecting a building, a carpenter must have an accurate plumb line; otherwise, the resulting structure could wind up to be a new Leaning Tower of Pisa. In your home, have you ever tried to hang wallpaper without a plumb line? What a disaster!

Similarly, in science all experimentation starts from the use of a "constant"—something sure, unmoving, unchanging—in order to arrive at consistently accurate conclusions. Without a reliable constant, the researcher can never be sure of his findings.

In the same way, we, too, must build our lives using a plumb line or a constant. The constant we choose must be true, trustworthy, and unchangeable.

Nowadays humanism tells us that everything is relative. That's a modern way of saying that happy lives can be built without plumb lines. When it comes to the things of God, to think in relative terms is sheer idiocy. Ask anyone who's tried it for a time.

As human beings we are walking variables, unpredictable; we're happy one moment, sad the next. There's nothing constant in our life—except when we make Christ, the living Word, our constant, our plumb line. Then we have direction and a straight path to guide us. He is the only constant of whom we can say, "[He] is the same yesterday and today and forever" (Hebrews 13:8).

We are the most blessed people on earth because we have truth as our plumb line. What a privilege to order our lives around His never-changing Word, which Jesus verified as truth in John 17:17 when He declared to the Father, "Your word is truth."

The Bible gives us a point of reference, a stake around which we must move in order to maintain stability in our lives. Whatever situation we find ourselves in, we can bounce our questions and concerns off the unchanging truth of God's Word in the same way that the scientist challenges the variables against the constant.

But even though our faith must have a reliable object, the Bible itself can never replace the true object of our faith. The Bible is *God's revelation of Jesus Christ*, the living Word.

Jesus reprimanded the Pharisees even though they knew the Old Testament Scriptures better than anyone else. All their lives these men had been schooled in Scripture. They had learned, memorized, repeated, taught, written, and spoken the verses about the coming Messiah ever since their youth. And yet, when He stood in front of them—Jesus Christ, their promised Messiah—they didn't recognize Him. Their study and knowledge didn't help them when the One of whom all their learning spoke stood before them. "You diligently study the Scriptures because you think that by them you possess eternal life. These are the Scriptures that testify about me, yet you refuse to come to Me to have life" (John 5:39,40).

The Pharisees knew the book, yet they missed the Author. We can make the same mistake. We all learned in school to read a book to learn the contents, not to know the author. And then as Christians, we carry that same mentality to our study of the Bible. We become students of the book but miss the Author. Jesus amplified this point further as He continued, "If you believed Moses, you would believe Me, for he wrote about Me. But since you do not believe what he wrote, how are you going to believe what I say?" (John 5:46,47).

Part of the problem with the Pharisees was that this man from Nazareth, Jesus Christ, was talking about "faith" as a way to please God. This concept was totally foreign to the Jews because they were depending on their obedience to the law to gain God's righteousness and favor. In their minds, they thought obedience to the law was God's desire for them. So when Jesus came and tried to make them see that God looks upon the heart and not outward behavior, they did not understand and saw no need for faith in Him.

Old Testament Faith

When we read the Old Testament, it's easy to see how the Pharisees could come to their conclusions.

In the entire Old Testament, which takes up 80 percent of the Bible, *faith* is mentioned only 15 times, and never in terms of a relationship with God. Mostly it refers to a man breaking faith with his wife or Israel breaking faith with their God.

The reason is that the object of the faith that pleases God—Jesus Christ, the Messiah—hadn't yet been revealed. God, through the prophets of old, talked about the day when He would come, and what He would accomplish for all mankind. And many of the saints of the Old Testament believed in the One who was prophesied to come. They were saved, if you will, on a credit card. They enjoyed some of the benefits of salvation, but they knew there would be a time in the future when the final payment for sin would be made and the full benefits of salvation would be available. We read about these saints in Hebrews 11. But this was the best they could do, not yet knowing the object of their faith. They couldn't have faith in Him yet because, as Paul says, faith had not yet been revealed. "But the Scripture declares that the whole world is a prisoner of sin, so that what was promised, being given through faith in Jesus Christ, might be given to those who believe. Before this faith came, we were held prisoners by the law, locked up until faith should be revealed" (Galatians 3:22,23).

Until faith is revealed to a person, all that person sees when he reads the Old Testament is law. He has the attitude of "Lord, just tell me what to do to gain eternal life, and I will do it." This is how the Israelites responded to Moses after he came down from Mount Sinai. They said, "We will do everything the LORD has said" (Exodus 19:8). And yet, before Moses could get off the mountain, they were having orgies and building a golden calf to a foreign god. They were blinded by their pride and deceived into thinking they could carry out the plan of God in the energy of the flesh.

As a matter of fact, Paul states, "Even to this day when Moses is read, a veil covers their hearts. But whenever anyone turns to the Lord, the veil is taken away" (2 Corinthians 3:15,16). One pastor I know said when he first started studying the Bible, someone told him to place a "c" next to all the commands, and a "p" next to all the promises. He said that after a while, he started getting "c" sick. If we don't realize that the purpose of the Bible is to point us to Christ, then all we will see are the dos and the don'ts.

The sad reality is that a person with this mind-set may know what the Word says, but will not have a clue as to what it means. We see this with the Pharisees. They knew what the Word said, but because faith had not been revealed to them, they didn't have a clue as to what it meant. For example, they read the Word and decided that they needed to work on their own righteousness through obedience to the law, rather than recognizing their inability to perfect themselves and their need to submit to the righteousness of God, which is by faith. They didn't question what the Word said. They just didn't know what it meant, so they leaned on their own understanding. And because they didn't know the meaning, they weren't sure how to respond to God.

So how can we understand what the Word means? Paul answers this question with these words: "'No eye has seen, no ear has heard, no mind has conceived what God has prepared for those who love him'—but God has revealed it to us by his Spirit" (1 Corinthians 2:9,10).

Can we rely on our intellect and education to understand the Word of God? No! Can we trust, as some people encourage us to do, in the science of biblical interpretation and an understanding of the original languages to glean the Bible's meaning? No! These are tools to help us know what the Bible says. But only the Spirit of God who lives in the believer can teach us what it means.

The work of the Spirit, therefore, is to point us to Jesus Christ. As we depend on Him, we will see the truth that Jesus proclaimed to the Pharisees: "All Scripture points to Me." This is so important to understand. Only as we see the message concerning Christ will we be able to respond with faith that pleases God. "Faith comes from hearing the message, and the message is heard through the word of Christ" (Romans 10:17).

This is why I encourage believers to spend the majority of their Bible study in the New Testament. Although it constitutes only 20 percent of the Bible, the New Testament gives us the full picture of Jesus Christ and what He has accomplished for us. In getting to know Him, we will see clearly how to respond to Him by faith.

The Colossians Had It Right

In chapter 2 we saw how those in the Galatian church had shifted their faith back to their previous way of life. They were rooted in legalism, and after the apostle Paul left their midst, they returned to legalism. Rather than walking by faith, they fell back to self-effort, trying to perfect themselves. In contrast, Paul commended the Colossian church for their walk of faith. He wrote these words to them: "We always thank God, the Father of our

Lord Jesus Christ, when we pray for you, because we have heard of your faith in Christ Jesus and of the love you have for all the saints" (Colossians 1:3,4).

Note that Paul isn't commending them for their faith, but for their *faith in Christ Jesus.* It was the object of their faith that Paul stressed.

As we saw in the last chapter, we can supplement or shift our faith to either performance or legalism, as did the Galatians, or we can suffer from misplaced faith.

Misplaced Faith

If the object of our faith isn't Christ, then we have misplaced our faith on a lesser object. Many people make foolish choices as to the object of their faith. Look around you and pay attention to the various objects of faith in which people are willing to trust.

Not too many years ago, a group of people put their faith in a "religion" that promised them that a spaceship would soon arrive and take them back to the mother planet. The result was a mass suicide similar to that of Jonestown—another sad episode where many people were led astray and convinced to put their faith in the words of a man. Such false teaching is widespread. But because men such as these are very persuasive, they have many followers. You don't have to look very far to find misplaced faith.

Down through history, sincere Christians have misplaced their faith by looking to powerful, charismatic leaders. Cults and sects have been started when unsuspecting people were lured away by enticing words and impressive speakers. In such cases, the object of faith becomes the man or the movement of the hour.

Even Christians who ought to know better can be swept up into movements that serve as substitutes for faith. One area where we see this happening today is in politics. Some earnest, well-meaning Christians believe that the solution to the world's problems is to elect all Christians into office (obviously, they have never been to a deacons' meeting). The object of their faith is to have their man in power—a man with high credentials and experience whom they think will solve the problems of this country. There is nothing wrong with our political leaders being Christians if they are living in a trust relationship with Christ, but they should never be the object of our faith.

For other people, the object of faith is faith itself. It is faith in faith. They view faith as a power by which they can gain success, wealth, and health. As we've learned, the value of faith is found in the object of that faith, *not in faith itself.*

Sadly, some Christians who are not rooted in the truth of the Word of God misplace their faith in activities, like I did. They know something vital is missing in their personal Christian life. They've recognized the symptoms of shifting faith, but they look in the wrong direction for the cure. In so doing, they become easy prey for false teachers.

The correct solution is to go back to step one and turn our faith back to the Son of God, to the One whom God has provided as the source for all our needs: "His divine power has given us everything we need for life and godliness" (2 Peter 1:3,4).

Jesus Christ, by His own words, has identified Himself as the source and fulfillment for all our needs—He is the Alpha and the Omega. In the Gospel of John, Jesus identified Himself as the "I am" in several ways.

> I am the bread of life. He who comes to Me will never go hungry, and he who believes in Me will never be thirsty (John 6:35).

> I am the light of the world. Whoever follows Me will never walk in darkness, but will have the light of life (John 8:12).

> I am the gate; whoever enters through Me will be saved. He will come in and go out, and find pasture (John 10:9).

> I am the good shepherd. The good shepherd lays down his life for the sheep (John 10:11).

> I am the resurrection and the life. He who believes in Me will live, even though he dies (John 11:25).

> I am the way and the truth and the life. No one comes to the Father except through Me (John 14:6).

> I am the vine; you are the branches. If a man remains in Me and I in him, he will bear much fruit; apart from Me you can do nothing (John 15:5).

In the verses above we see that Christ offers everything that our heart longs for and desires. There is no one in this world more worthy than Jesus, and there is nothing that compares to knowing Him by faith.

As we place our total being on Him and on Him alone, we will experience a faith that has roots; a faith that brings joy, peace, and rest; a faith that pleases God.

Faith: Initiator or Responder?

As I HAVE LOOKED BACK on the day I received Christ, I've learned some valuable lessons about the true nature of faith. God foresaw my need before time began and initiated a plan whereby I could know Him and be saved. He didn't consult me about that plan. He didn't ask my permission to put it into effect. He simply took the initiative to send His Son to die on my behalf and to offer me His resurrected life. When I heard the gospel that day, my only options were either to respond by faith and receive His life or to reject the offer. Some people who hear the gospel choose to reject God's gift. But the faith I exercised that day was merely a response to something that originated entirely with God. He took the initiative; I responded.

Herein lies the definition of faith: *Faith is man's response to what God has already initiated on his behalf.*

God is always the initiator. We are responders. When you truly think about it, this is the way it must be. It just makes sense that God initiates and man responds.

God is all-powerful, omniscient, independent, merciful, righteous, holy, and just. He "calls into being that which does not exist" (Romans 4:17 NASB). He is the creator of all things. He has always been, and He is perfect love.

The apostle Paul says this of God: "The God who made the world and all things in it, since He is Lord of heaven and earth, does not dwell in temples made with hands; neither is He served by human hands, as though He needed anything, since He Himself gives to all life and breath and all things" (Acts 17:24,25 NASB).

Man, on the other hand, was created to be dependent, not independent. God alone is the independent One. We were created to respond to God. When we refuse to live in dependency upon our Creator, we are forced to shift our dependency to the things of this world.

Genesis 2:7 describes how we came into being: "The LORD God formed the man from the dust of the ground and breathed into his nostrils the breath of life, and the man became a living being." In spite of these humble beginnings, man in his pride and ego thinks he can be like God.

The Christian world today suffers from what I like to call spiritual dyslexia. In our minds, we have reversed the roles—we see ourselves as initiators and God as a responder. This spiritual dyslexia has reached epidemic proportions.

Faith or Manipulation?

Many well-meaning Christians believe that their faith causes things to happen. But in reality, God wants us to respond to His will and put our faith in what He has already done. Our faith responds to the totality of what God has accomplished on our behalf through Christ Jesus, *but our faith is never the cause of it.*

Think about it. If we believe our faith can cause God to do something, then we are saying in essence that we are greater and wiser than God. We know what is good, but He has to pull it off for us. We have reversed roles— we initiate; God responds.

There is a principle commonly known as the "law of causality," which says that the effect of something is never greater than the cause. For example, the heat from the sun isn't greater than the sun. In the spiritual world, the gift is never greater than the Giver. Grace isn't greater than God. My salvation is not greater than my Savior.

When we become the initiator and think of Him as the responder, we're saying that we have become like God. This is an impossibility, but it's the way the enemy of our soul wants us to think and approach our relationship with God. That was his temptation to Adam and Eve in the Garden of Eden, and he is still tempting us in the same way today. This fallacy, which is one of the major attractions of the so-called "faith movement," says that I can cause God to do anything I want Him to do. In reality, it's nothing more than trying to sway and manipulate God to our way of thinking.

This heresy is based on the pride of man. We want to be the big shots, the initiators. We want to be in control and make all the decisions, and then ask God to bless us. As initiators, we are in control. Remember Satan's words to Eve in the Garden of Eden: "God knows that in the day you eat from [the tree] your eyes will be opened, and you will be like God" (Genesis 3:5 NASB). The temptation to Adam and Eve was that they could be the god of their own lives and differentiate between good and evil without consulting God. No longer would they need to depend on and trust in their Creator. We fall prey to this same deception, and in so doing become the initiator and see God as the responder.

All of us can probably think of ways we have tried to initiate a response from God. In my own life, I was trying to sway God into action when I was sitting in that hospital chapel, promising God I would dedicate my life to Him if He would get my dad well again. What about the prayer chains that are common in Christian circles? We don't believe that the prayer of one person will be effective, so we get as many people as we can presenting the same request to God, hoping that He will respond. Every one of us could recite examples like these of how we've tried to get God to answer our prayers.

Think about this: We are willing to trust God with our eternal life, but when it comes to our day-to-day lives here on earth, we are doubtful. So we charge ahead. After all, we know what we want and what's best for us. Oh, we may not say it out loud, but our gut feeling must be right. But in retrospect, we see how our eagerness to have things go our way has landed us in trouble that could have been avoided if we had only trusted God and waited upon Him.

I see this quite often in marriages. Mary called our radio program one night seeking help. She had been married for a year when her husband filed for divorce. Mary was devastated and didn't know what to do. Her story was typical. She had wanted to get married, and she wasn't going to be happy until that day arrived. She met Jim, an attractive guy who really struck her fancy. After a few dates, she started to think, "This must be the one."

During the courtship, Mary discovered that Jim was not a Christian. But she knew that he was the one for her and that somehow God would bring Jim around. Even though in God's Word it clearly says to not be unequally yoked with an unbeliever, Mary had determined that marrying Jim was best for her. Like many people, she was more in love with the idea of marriage than with the man she was marrying. She was fearful, too, that if she let Jim get away, she might never get married. She bought her wedding dress, and when the date arrived, she lived out her wedding fantasy. But the day after the honeymoon, the relationship started to fall apart. It had really started to fall apart long before the wedding day, but Mary didn't heed the warnings. After a year, she was going through a tragic divorce as a result of her "ideal" man becoming a wife-beater.

I can't tell you the number of people I have counseled who have experienced the same story, all because of an unwillingness to trust the Lord and recognize that He knows best when He says, "Do not be yoked together with unbelievers" (2 Corinthians 6:14).

The faith that pleases God recognizes that there's no area of our life that God hasn't considered. He knows our past, He knows our present, and He knows our future. He knows every hidden motive of our heart and every thought. And because He is a God who loves us, He has initiated a unique plan for our happiness. When we *respond* to God and learn to walk by faith in Him, we live contented, productive lives—even in the midst of seeming adversity.

Faith is believing that God knows best and is faithful, even when we are faithless. This attitude of trust toward God results in the peace of God and rest for the believer.

Second Peter 1:3 tells us that God has given us "everything we need for life and godliness through our knowledge of him who called us by his own glory and good-   ness." How then are we by our self-effort going to get more from God, when He clearly tells us that we've already been given all we need for life? "Everything" means it's ours already when we come to Him. We access by faith all He has provided.

By the way, this underscores the importance of believers continuing to grow in their knowledge of Jesus Christ and in their understanding of what He says in His Word. We must understand the foundational truths of the faith because those truths are what we're to access as we grow. If you don't know who God is and His character and what He has already done and prepared for His children, then you can't access what is yours.

God's Truth Requires a Response

Some facts are interesting information, but they don't require a response from us. For example, we learn in school that Abraham Lincoln was elected president in 1860 and that he was assassinated in 1865. That's true—that's a fact. But does it require a response from us? Not really.

With God's truth, it's different. His facts require a response. For example, we read earlier in John 8:12 that Jesus claimed to be "the light of the world. Whoever follows me will never walk in darkness, but will have the light of life." Notice He didn't stop with His claim to be the light of the world. This isn't just a fact He wants us to know or an interesting bit of trivia, but a truth to be believed and experienced. God's desire for us is that we know Him and have Him as our light and our guide in life. We respond to this truth, knowing that in Him we will never walk in darkness.

Every promise God initiates in His Word is for us to take and trust in. His storehouse of promises is full. All we have to do is respond by faith. God took the initiative to show us His love. As we respond to that love, we will see our love for Him growing in our hearts. We can't muster up a love for God through our own strength. No, as John so clearly states, "We love because He first loved us....This is love: not that we loved God, but that he loved us and sent his Son as an atoning sacrifice for our sins" (1 John 4:19,10).

Here we see again and again God as the initiator and ourselves as responders.

Christ: Our Example

Jesus demonstrated to us this life of faith while here on earth. Although He was and is and always will be God, when He was on earth He lived as a man. In so doing, He taught us how we are to live.

For example, Jesus said, "I tell you the truth, the Son can do nothing by himself; he can do only what he sees his Father doing, because whatever the Father does the Son also does" (John 5:19). Jesus did not initiate His own independent actions. He waited and responded to His Father's initiation.

A few verses later Jesus again shows us His dependency on God by adding, "By myself I can do nothing; I judge only as I hear, and my judgment is just, for I seek not to please myself but him who sent me" (John 5:30). In another place He said, "For I did not speak of my own accord, but the Father who sent me commanded me what to say and how to say it" (John 12:49). Jesus healed the sick because the Father told Him to. He multiplied the loaves and fish to feed the masses because the Father told Him to. He taught the disciples because the Father told Him to. He didn't do any of these things of His own initiative. He simply responded to what His Father was telling Him to do. He lived in total dependency on His Father in every detail of His earthly life. And incidentally, He said to us, "As the Father has sent me, so send I you."

This then is how we are to live: in total dependence upon Jesus in every detail of our lives. Paul wrote, "Your attitude should be the same as that of Christ Jesus" (Philippians 2:5). Notice, He said *attitude*, not *action*. Many Christians live with the idea that they should imitate Jesus. They say, "If Jesus were here, what would He do?" Some Christians wear a wristband with the initials WWJD? which stand for "What would Jesus do?" This sounds noble, and I'm sure the promoters of this are well-meaning in their desire to encourage people to live a Christ-centered life. But the answer to "What would Jesus do?" is that He did what the Father told Him to do. However, what the Father told Jesus to do is not necessarily what He will tell you and me to do. I personally have never been told to feed 5,000 people or to raise the dead or to walk on water. These things the Father told Jesus to do, not me.

As Jesus walked in dependence on His Father, we are to walk in dependence on Him. Our actions will be an outflow of our attitudes. If we are trusting in Christ and are willing to respond to His leading, then we never have to worry about what we should do. Jesus' example to us

was a life of responding to and deper
who loves us the most.

Bewitched Christiaɪ

Some Christians begin their Chris
readily responding to the free gift of life that Christ
offers. But soon that old religious flesh raises its head
and insists on getting into action, doing something for
God. Remember the Galatians I mentioned in chapter 2?
Though they began well by faith alone, they later
insisted on commingling some law into their faith. In no
uncertain terms Paul rebuked them. "You foolish Galatians! Who has bewitched you?" he asked in Galatians
3:1. He then goes on to ask them a question about how
they began their Christian life: "by observing the law, or
by believing what you heard? Are you so foolish? After
beginning with the Spirit, are you now trying to attain
your goal by human effort?" (verses 2-3).

Today, the average Christian lives his Christian life
just as the Galatians did. He comes to Christ by faith and
then gets involved and busy trying to please the Lord
through self-effort. As my wife would say, "We have
started listening to the sheep, rather than the Shepherd!
And the sheep will run us ragged." Oftentimes, what the
sheep tell us to do is not what God has in mind at all.

For example, have you ever heard anyone say to a
new Christian, "Let's spend the next three months
learning about what Jesus has done for you"? I sure
haven't. More likely we hear something like, "Okay,
now that you have become a Christian, here's what you
need to do: You need to read your Bible every day. You
better start having a quiet time. Be sure and start to tithe

ncome. You need to get out and witness to other ple." These suggestions are not bad in and of themselves but too often they become a substitute for first building into a new believer a trust relationship with Christ. A new Christian can start on this path of performance all excited and enthusiastic, but soon the joy is replaced with fatigue. The words of Paul ring in our ears: "You foolish Christians, who has bewitched you?"

The Christian life is not to be lived through self-effort in obedience to the law, but by faith as we are led internally by the Spirit of God. The reason people insist on hanging onto the law is that they have never experienced being led by the Spirit. It thus becomes easy to fall into the trap of being an initiator instead of a responder. But that's not God's plan nor His desire for us. He will not keep us wandering in the wilderness if we allow ourselves to be led by Him.

The Christian life is a life of faith from beginning to end. The faith in Christ that first saved us is the same faith by which we grow and live. "So then, just as you received Christ Jesus as Lord, continue to live in him, rooted and built up in him, strengthened in the faith as you were taught, and overflowing with thankfulness" (Colossians 2:6,7).

How did you receive Christ Jesus as Lord? By faith. So how are you to continue to live in Him? By that same faith. As we are rooted and built up in Christ, we will experience hearts that overflow with thankfulness. What other attitude could we have when we are responding to all that Christ has accomplished for us? Our proper response of thankfulness to God's gift of grace changes us as we see how grace provides for us what we could never provide for ourselves.

Thankfulness Leads to
a Conviction of Truth

Sometimes in our lives there are spells of smooth sailing. At other times, there are fierce, raging storms that threaten to sink us. The writer of Hebrews tells us about some people who "conquered kingdoms, administered justice…who shut the mouths of lions, quenched the fury of the flames" (Hebrews 11:33-34). We read this and think, "That's amazing!" But the writer goes on to talk about other people who were stoned, sawed in two, and put to death in other ways. And yet, to both groups he said that the Lord commended them for their faith. Regardless of our circumstances, when we learn to live trusting God and overflowing with thankfulness, we begin to develop a strong conviction of what we believe. As we experience His faithfulness, our faith deepens. And as that conviction is internalized, we develop an attitude of continually abiding in Him.

We see this in the apostle Paul. What he went through for the sake of the gospel is beyond comprehension. He endured hardships of every kind from the time of his conversion to the day he was "absent from the body and present with the Lord." It would have been very easy to doubt the reality of God's love, yet Paul persevered and continued to trust the risen Christ. Through every trial, through every hardship, the reality of God's love deepened in his heart to the point that near the end of His life he could write, "For I am convinced that neither death nor life, neither angels nor demons, neither the present nor the future, nor any powers, neither height nor depth, nor anything else in all creation, will be able to separate us from the love of God that is in Christ Jesus our Lord" (Romans 8:38,39).

These weren't just mere words for Paul. In every situation he faced, he continued to respond by faith to the truth of God's love and grace. His response led to a deep conviction of the heart. This is God's desire for all of us. Like Paul, as we become convinced of God's love, we, too, will experience great peace and a life of total rest in Him.

We've all known some Christians who have this quality. Usually they don't talk much about their lot in life. It's a very personal thing, unique to each individual. But what they will tell you is that the peace they have has come through abiding in Christ. By abiding, they've experienced the peace of God that passes all understanding. And that's God's goal for each of us—not to fear the past, the present, nor the future, but to be assured of His presence at the time of need.

The day a person accepts Christ by faith, that initial response is just the beginning of a life of faith that's constantly building more conviction and character in a believer which results in more abiding.

I liken accepting Christ to walking through a gate into a lush garden. You can see that what's ahead is beautiful, but you don't stop admiring it at the gate. Instead, you move on and respond in wonder to all that is before you. So, too, we respond daily with thanks for all that God has given.

Once you've entered the gate, keep walking by faith. Keep responding to all that God offers. And keep thanking Him for who He is and for all He's done. The faith that pleases God is not in us, but in Him.

Responding to God's Offer of Life

ONE OF THE TRUTHS WE SEE over and over in the Bible is that God offers salvation to everyone. To every person, rich or poor, young or old, man or woman, boy or girl, God says, "Come." The wonderful thing about salvation is that it is available to whosoever will. God shows no partiality.

Some people hear the message of the gospel but never really catch or understand the deep meaning of what they're hearing. Because they misunderstand what salvation is, they don't know how to respond. I was that way for the first 36 years of my life. But when I found out exactly what God's offer was, I also discovered why faith in Jesus Christ is the only thing that pleases God.

So what exactly *is* God's offer to man? Is it a fire-insurance policy to keep a person from going to hell and experiencing eternal damnation and punishment? Is it a means whereby a person can escape and overcome his or her present troubles? Is it so that we can become better people? John 20:31 gives us the answer when the Gospel writer tells why he wrote his account: "But these are written that you may believe that Jesus is the Christ, the Son of God, and that by believing *you may have life in his name*" (emphasis added).

God's offer to humanity is *life*. Why does He offer us His life? Because we are born spiritually dead. No matter what our problems may be, without spiritual life we are lost and our deepest need is new life, which is only in Christ Jesus.

The truth about mankind is this: Everyone comes into this world spiritually dead, separated from the life of God. This condition is the result of sin, which took place in the garden through Adam and Eve.

The Significance of Adam's Sin

God created Adam in His own image. However, since the Fall, there has been an infinite gulf between God and man. God is the only truly independent one. He is totally self-sufficient and, therefore, needs nothing. Man, on the other hand, is a totally *dependent* creature. He is dependent on air, food, water, etc. for his physical life. He is dependent on the world around him and other people for his soulish well-being; and he is dependent on God for his spiritual life. In particular, man was created with a need for unconditional love and acceptance, meaning and purpose in life. Man's spiritual emptiness or vacuum can only be filled through God's Spirit coming to live in him and so making him complete.

The key to the real meaning of the temptation presented to Adam and Eve lies in the serpent's phrase "when you eat of it...you will be like God" (Genesis 2:5).

They were offered the chance (they thought) to step outside of their dependent (faith) relationship with God and to assume an independent status—to be their own gods, to be self-sufficient.

In effect, Satan was saying, "You can get along without God. You can be your own god, determining right from wrong. You can decide for yourself what is good and evil, and you can start right now by asserting your independence!"

The Results of Adam's Sin

Notice that God said, "In the day that you eat from it you shall surely die" (Genesis 2:17 NASB). Adam and Eve did not die *physically* that day. In fact, we're told that Adam lived a total of 930 years. However, by believing Satan and calling God a liar, Adam and Eve died *spiritually* that day. God created humanity not to be robots, but to be free to choose. So He honored their choice to live independently from Him. He withdrew His life from them, leaving them dead spiritually and on their own. The enticing promise of the serpent was a lie. When God withdrew His Spirit, Adam and Eve lost their spiritual life, and a void and emptiness took over.

When Adam and Eve had children, their offspring inherited their parents' fallen nature. You can see this in Genesis 5:1,3: "When God created man, he made him in the likeness of God…When Adam had lived 130 years, he had a son in his own likeness, in his own image; and he named him Seth." The rule of reproduction is "Like begets like," and two spiritually dead, sinful parents can only produce spiritually dead, sinful children. Adam could not pass on what he no longer had: spiritual life.

Romans chapter 5 simplifies this truth: "Therefore, just as sin entered the world through one man, and death through sin, and in this way death came to all men, because all sinned...as the result of one trespass was condemnation for all men...as through the disobedience of the one man the many were made sinners" (Romans 5:12,18,19).

As a result of Adam's choice, every person is born into this world spiritually dead—for the wages of sin is death—and a sinner by nature. The apostle Paul tells us,

> As for you, you were dead in your transgressions and sins, in which you used to live when you followed the ways of this world and of the ruler of the kingdom of the air, the spirit who is now at work in those who are disobedient. All of us also lived among them at one time, gratifying the cravings of our sinful nature and following its desires and thoughts. Like the rest, we were by nature objects of wrath (Ephesians 2:1-3).

Therefore, from God's point of view, the problem of mankind isn't just that we are sinners who need forgiveness; He sees a world of dead people who need life.

Many of us miss the offer of God's life because we don't see our true condition. It would be rather silly to walk into a graveyard and ask, "Hey, do you dead people need any help?" A corpse doesn't need help. He needs *life!* He needs resurrection life. That's why faith in Jesus Christ is the *only* thing that pleases God, because Jesus is the only One who can give life.

When we "received Christ" as our Savior at the moment of our conversion, what of Christ did we receive? It was His very life, wasn't it? Consider these three verses from John's Gospel that tell us that we have been given *life* by Christ:

> For just as the Father raises the dead and gives them life, even so the Son gives life to whom he is pleased to give it (John 5:21).
>
> You diligently study the Scriptures because you think that by them you possess eternal life. These are the Scriptures that testify about me, yet you refuse to come to Me to have life (John 5:39-40).
>
> I have come that they may have life, and have it to the full (John 10:10).

Remember, that's what John said later in his letter— that the purpose of his writing was that the reader might have life. The ultimate result of believing the gospel is the impartation of eternal life. We have *eternal* life because we are in the *eternal* One. This truth is what distinguishes Christianity from every other religion or philosophy. Hinduism, Buddhism, or any other "ism" you can think of offers only concepts such as self-actualization or ethical and moral codes to follow. Some people may even live better lives on this earth by following these religions, but none of them offers a solution to the real need of man: new life. Religion can't provide spiritual life. It cannot answer the question, "What happens when we die?"

Many people see Christianity as too dogmatic. They believe there are many ways to God and that we should be more tolerant in our viewpoint. However, this isn't a dogmatic doctrine. This is reality. Buddha can't offer us life. Muhammad can't offer us life. Neither can following strict moral or ethical codes or a particular philosophy earn eternal life. Only Christ can give life freely by grace.

The reason He can give life is that He's the only One with a life to give. Consider all the facts concerning His birth. When the angel appeared to Mary, he said to her, "You will be with child and give birth to a son, and you are to give him the name Jesus." In response Mary asked, "How will this be, since I am a virgin?" The angel answered, "The Holy Spirit will come upon you, and the power of the Most High will overshadow you. So the holy one to be born will be called the Son of God" (Luke 1:31-35). The angel confirmed this to Joseph as well. "Joseph...do not be afraid to take Mary home as your wife, because what is conceived in her is from the Holy Spirit" (Matthew 1:20).

Christ wasn't born into the world like the rest of us. We were born of natural descent, of human passion and plan. He was conceived of the Holy Spirit and born of a virgin. The doctrine of the virgin birth isn't up for grabs. It had to be that way, otherwise He would have come into the world just like us: from the loins of Adam, dead spiritually. But because of His miraculous birth, He came into the world totally alive—bodily, soulishly, and spiritually. Adam was created alive spiritually. Jesus was born into the world alive spiritually. He was the first one in human form since Adam to have spiritual life and is therefore referred to in Scripture as the "last Adam."

Earlier in this chapter we talked about Adam and Eve and how their sin brought death to all men. But the wonderful "good news" is this: "So it is written: 'The first man Adam became a living being'; *the last Adam, a life-giving spirit*" (1 Corinthians 15:45, emphasis added).

Throughout the New Testament writings, we read promises regarding this new life Christ offers. In Romans 4:17, the apostle Paul, in speaking of Abraham—a man who was certainly not perfect, but who responded to God in faith—says he is "our father in the sight of God, in whom he believed—the God who gives life to the dead."

Consider also these words of Paul regarding life:

> For, if when we were God's enemies, we were reconciled to him through the death of his Son, how much more, having been reconciled, shall we be saved through his life! (Romans 5:10).

> For you died, and your life is now hidden with Christ in God. When Christ, who is your life, appears, then you also will appear with him in glory (Colossians 3:3,4).

> Paul, an apostle of Christ Jesus by the will of God, according to the promise of life that is in Christ Jesus (2 Timothy 1:1).

These are just a few of the many New Testament verses that testify to the "life" of the believer—the life that is in the Son. If you are a Christian, you already have this *eternal* life, which can never be taken away from you.

Through Christ's death we were saved from our sins, but through His resurrection, we're given the gift of righteousness and eternal life. After paying the price for the sins of the world, Jesus was resurrected to life. And that life—*resurrection life*—is now made available to all who believe in Him.

Among Christians, we focus mostly on Christ's death for our sins, and certainly His death is critical in that it took away our sins. But as Paul admonishes us in 1 Corinthians, the resurrection is key to the validity of Christianity: "And if Christ has not been raised, your faith is futile; you are still in your sins" (1 Corinthians 15:17).

Many so-called learned theologians dispute some of the cardinal doctrines of the faith, including the deity of Christ and His resurrection. But if Jesus wasn't born of divine means, then He has no divine life to offer us. And if He didn't really rise from the dead, then we can't be partakers of His resurrection life. If such is the case, we are without hope. Paul amplifies this when he writes, "If Christ has not been raised, our preaching is useless and so is your faith" (1 Corinthians 15:14).

Man, then, is not saved by the death of Christ, but by the *life* of Christ. Before Adam and Eve sinned, they enjoyed communion with God, and through our new resurrection life in Christ, we find that the relationship of communion with God is restored. We once again enjoy fellowship with God.

The Spirit of God now lives in the born-again believer in Christ. And God living in man is indispensable to the true humanity of man as God designed him to be. It was God's ultimate act of love and sovereignty to redeem that which was lost.

And what a provision of redemption He initiated! Through Christ, His only begotten Son, God has made a way for His life to be injected back into man—a restoration of His original intent for mankind. And even better is the assurance that this has been accomplished in such a way that mankind can never again lose His life.

Why?

Because Christ is eternal and it is impossible to lose what is eternal. If His life can be lost, it's not eternal. At the cross, Jesus took away forever that which causes spiritual death: sin. Sin is what caused God's life to depart from Adam. Sin is what caused the life to depart from the physical Jesus. Christ dealt with sin at the cross forever. He took away all sins—past, present, and future—for all people. He has removed them away from us as far as the east is from the west. That being the case, there is nothing that could cause us to lose our spiritual life. That which causes us to lose it—sin—has been dealt with *forever.*

That, my friend, is the meaning of the cross and the victory of the cross. The cross is the place where God cleared the deck for the divine action of bringing life to the dead. The eternal act of forgiveness at the cross is what enables us to have eternal life. "In Him we have redemption through His blood, the forgiveness of sins, in accordance with the riches of God's grace" (Ephesians 1:7). We don't *get* forgiveness; we *have* it.

Consider the importance of Jesus' words to Martha at the death of her brother, Lazarus: "I am the resurrection and the life. He that believeth in Me, though he were dead, yet shall he live. Do you believe this?" (John 11:25,26, KJV).

The powerful thunder of His words resounds through the centuries—words still being asked of every human being: *"Do you believe this?"* If the answer is yes, then *you will never die another spiritual death.* You now and forever have eternal life. As John quotes Jesus in John 5:24, "I tell you the truth, whoever hears My word and believes Him who sent Me has eternal life and will not be condemned; he has crossed over from death to life."

This truth is so magnificent it is sometimes hard for people to grasp. It sounds too good to be true that we could be saved forever, that we who are so undeserving could actually have eternal life.

Since it takes us a long time to comprehend the completeness of what Christ has done, we often view salvation like rescuing a drowning man. First, we think people will be saved simply by following our good example. But to a drowning man, someone swimming alongside showing him how to swim isn't going to help. Can you imagine jumping into the water and saying, "Watch me. Here's how you swim"? And when you look back at the desperate soul, you see him going under the water for the last time.

Or sometimes we think education may be the way to salvation. Again, can you imagine throwing the drowning man a book and telling him, "Here, read this. It'll show you how to swim"? And again he goes under the water and disappears.

No, to save the drowning person, you jump out of the boat, grab the guy, and pull him into the boat. But even this may not result in salvation. Let's say that on the way to shore, he starts to cuss at you for taking so long to get him out of the water, and then he even has the nerve to ask for a cigarette. This makes you so mad at him that you just pitch him back into the water. Would you call this act salvation? No, of course not. He didn't receive salvation, just a reprieve. Salvation can't be anything short of seeing a man drowning, pulling him into the boat, and delivering him safely to shore. That's salvation. Anything short of that is a reprieve. And God *saves* us completely. He doesn't give us a reprieve. He gives us *life* eternal in exchange for our spiritual death.

We once were dead in our sins, but God made us alive. He initiated the miracle of salvation. He got into the boat and came out to where we were flailing about in the water, drowning. He pulled us into the boat and delivered us safely to the shore. In fact, we are told that God has already "seated us with Him in the heavenly realms in Christ Jesus" (Ephesians 2:6).

You can know that you have eternal life and rest assured you will never lose it, not because of what you do, but because of what He did. To lose eternal life would mean you would have to lose Jesus, and He has promised that He "will never leave you nor forsake you" (Joshua 1:5).

You and I were dead. We needed life. The power that raised Jesus from the dead raised us to eternal life. God's offer is, "I have come so that you might have life." When we respond by faith and receive His life, we can know with confidence that we are in Christ and that seeing us in Him pleases God. We have accepted the free gift of His Son—the gift He was pleased to offer. And in the Son we have everything we need for life and godliness. The story that best illustrates this is called "Who Will Take the Son?"

"Who Will Take the Son?"

A wealthy man and his son loved to collect rare works of art. They had a large collection—everything from Picasso to Raphael. They would often sit together and admire the great masterpieces.

When the Vietnam War broke out, the son went to war. He was very courageous and died in battle while rescuing another soldier. The father was notified and grieved deeply for his only son.

About a month later, just before Christmas, there was a knock at the door. A young man stood there with a large package in his hands. He said, "Sir, you don't know me, but I am the soldier for whom your son gave his life. He saved many lives that day, and he was carrying me to safety when a bullet struck him in the heart, and he died instantly. In our conversations together, he often talked about you, and your love for art." The young man held out the package. "I know this isn't much. I'm not really a great artist, but I think your son would have wanted you to have this."

The father opened the package. It was a portrait of his son, painted by the young man. He stared in awe at the way the soldier had captured the true personality of his son in the painting. The father was so moved and drawn to the eyes of his son that his own eyes welled up with tears. He thanked the young man and offered to pay him for the picture. "Oh no, sir. I could never repay what your son did for me. It's a gift."

The father hung the portrait over the mantel. Every time visitors came to his home, he first showed them the portrait of his son before he showed them the other great works he had collected.

A few months later, the man died. There was to be a great auction of his paintings. Many influential people gathered, excited over seeing the magnificent works and having the opportunity to purchase one for their collection.

On the platform stood the easel with the painting of the son. The auctioneer pounded his gavel. "We will start the bidding with this picture titled, 'The Son.' Who will bid for this one?" There was silence. Then a voice in the back of the room shouted, "We want to see the famous paintings first. Skip this one."

But the auctioneer persisted. "Is there someone who will bid for this painting? Who will start the bidding? One hundred dollars? Two hundred dollars?"

From the back another voice shouted angrily, "We didn't come to see an unknown artist's work. We came to see the van Goghs, the Rembrandts—works of the masters. Get on with the real bids!"

But still the auctioneer continued. "'The Son!' 'The Son!' Who will take 'The Son'?" Finally, a raspy voice came from the very back of the room. It was the aged, longtime gardener of the man and his son. "I'll give ten dollars for the painting." Being a poor man, it was all he could afford.

"We have ten dollars. Who will bid twenty dollars?" asked the auctioneer.

"Give it to him for ten dollars," someone shouted. "Let's go on and see the paintings of the masters."

"Ten dollars is the bid. Won't someone bid twenty dollars?" the auctioneer persisted.

The crowd was becoming restless and angry. They didn't want the picture of the son. They wanted a more worthy and important investment for their collection.

The auctioneer pounded the gavel. "Going once, twice, sold for ten dollars!"

A man sitting on the second row shouted, "Now let's get on with the collection!"

But the auctioneer laid down his gavel. "I'm sorry. The auction is over," he said.

"What about the paintings?" someone shouted from the crowd.

"I'm sorry, but when I was called to conduct this auction, I was told of a secret stipulation in the will. And I was not allowed to reveal that stipulation until now. Only the painting of the son would be auctioned. Whoever bought that painting would inherit the entire estate, including the paintings. The man who took 'The Son' gets everything!"

God gave His Son 2,000 years ago to die on a cruel cross. Much like the auctioneer, His message today is, "The Son! The Son! Who will take the Son?"

You see, whoever takes the Son inherits everything.

John wrote these words: "And this is the testimony: God has given us eternal life, and this life is in His Son. He who has the Son has life; he who does not have the Son of God does not have life" (1 John 5:11,12).

We are talking about faith that pleases God. Let me ask you a question. Are you in Christ? Do you have the Son? If the answer is yes, then I ask you another question. Do you have life? What kind of life did Jesus offer you: eternal or temporal? If indeed He offered you eternal life, and if indeed you have received eternal life, what kind of life is yours eternally?

One more question for the road. Would it be faith for you as a born-again, redeemed believer to ask God to give you eternal life? Why not? The answer is that you have the Son, and because you have the Son, you have eternal life. In the next chapter I will prove to you why we can't lose our eternal life. So keep reading—there's more good news ahead.

6
Responding to the New Covenant

THE BEST DEFINITION THE BIBLE gives of *faith* is found in the book of Hebrews: "Now faith is the substance of things hoped for, the evidence of things not seen" (Hebrews 11:1 KJV).

Faith is the substance and faith is the evidence. Substance is something that comes and stands underneath us. It's a support, the solid rock on which we build our life.

The object of our faith—Jesus—is also described by the writer of Hebrews as "the exact representation of [God's] being" (Hebrews 1:3). In Jesus is everything we need to know about God. When we come to know Jesus, we know God and His character because Jesus Christ is the very *substance* of God. This is the same word used in the definition of *faith* above. When we have something of substance upholding us, like a strong foundation under a house, we're going to have confidence and security in life. And confidence is what we lack when we place our faith in anything that is flimsy, fleeting, and ever-changing, and has no substance to it.

The Greek word translated *evidence* literally means not just factual evidence, but the carrying out of those facts. The writer was trying to make sure the Hebrews understood that faith wasn't just intellectual assent to a set of facts, but putting those facts into action, internalizing, digging deep into what they said they believed. James emphasizes this in his letter when he states that believers must be "doers of the word, and not hearers only" (James 1:22 KJV).

Faith is a living word, not a static word. The implication from God's point of view is that faith is meant to be alive, vital, and solid. For that to be true, the object of our faith must be alive, vital, solid, unchanging, and eternal.

The New Testament book of Hebrews not only defines faith, but also reveals the object of the Christian's faith. In Hebrews, the mystery of Christ and His new covenant is unveiled.

The Gospel According to Hebrews

If I was given only one chance in my lifetime to deliver a message to a group of people, it would be the magnificent truth regarding the new covenant. This truth has been key to my understanding of faith and growth in the Christian life. As I've ministered to other people, it's been the key that has unlocked the reality of God's grace in the lives of literally thousands of believers.

The new covenant is important because it puts together all the pieces of the puzzle called the Christian life. For example, most Christians have an understanding of the doctrines of the faith such as righteousness, justification, eternal life, sanctification, and identity, but they don't know where these fit in the big picture and how they apply to their daily walk. For most people, these are just nebulous doctrines dangling out in space somewhere, as if they don't belong or connect to each other.

Historically, some groups have been so focused on individual doctrines that great division has resulted. New denominations and sects have been formed based on single doctrines taken from the new covenant. In the process, the true meaning of the doctrine and its place in the new covenant has been totally obscured.

But from God's point of view the issue isn't about a single dangling doctrine, but about His new covenant in its entirety. He doesn't ask, "What do you think about eternal life?" or "How do you stand on sanctification?" His question would be, "Are you in the new covenant, or are you still under the old?" The new covenant encompasses all that Jesus Christ has done and accomplished for you and me. *Everything.* That's why it's of utmost importance for every believer to understand the new covenant.

In order to fully understand this covenant, we need to begin at the place where it began—at the cross. The cross of Christ is the dividing line of all human history from God's point of view. The people of the world, even though they don't believe in Jesus Christ as Savior, still divide history by His coming to earth. They divide history as B.C.—before Christ was born, and A.D.—anno Domini, which translates into "the year of the Lord."

But from God's vantage point, it is not when Jesus was born that's most significant, but when He died. Human history should really be divided by B.C., "before the cross," and A.D., which is, as I jokingly say, an Italian term which means "after de cross." That's how God divides human history. But let's see if that's just a "Bob Georgism" or if it's scriptural.

"In the Case of a Will"

Hebrews 9:16,17 says, "In the case of a will, it is necessary to prove the death of the one who made it, because a will is in force only when somebody has died; it never takes effect while the one who made it is living."

Some of you have gone to a lawyer and had a will drawn up authorizing certain things to be done with your estate when you die. Now, when will that will take effect? On the day you *die*. And not one day before, not an hour before, not even a minute before.

Have you ever had more than one will drawn up during your life? If so, which one will go into effect when you die?

The last one, right? What about the ones you had drawn up previously and then changed as the years passed? Will they have any bearing on what goes to your heirs once you die?

No. Your children might go to the lawyer once you've passed away and plead, "Mr. Lawyer, I know Dad wanted me to have the Cadillac."

The lawyer will answer, "I'm sorry, but the Cadillac isn't in his last will."

Your son might say, "Yeah, I realize that, but did you read the one before his last one?"

"Yes, I did," the lawyer answers.

"Was the Cadillac in there?" your son asks.

"Yes, it was," the lawyer admits.

"Well," your son answers, "you know my dad is the same yesterday, today, and forever. He never changes, so he meant for me to have it. He must have just forgotten to put it in the last will."

Exasperated, the attorney will say, "I'm going to tell you for the last time, *the Cadillac is not yours*. It's not in the final will."

"But sir…"

"No arguments, please. There's no Cadillac mentioned in the will for you. Only what is in the last will is valid and will be passed on to you. End of discussion."

Friend, your beneficiaries are only going to inherit what you've outlined for them in your most recent will. And they will only inherit those things *after you die*. A will never takes effect until a person dies. And in our case, we're talking about a *new* will, a new agreement between God and man that went into effect when Jesus died on the cross, and not a moment before.

As the writer of Hebrews continues, he establishes a foundational premise that's crucial for us to understand:

> When Moses had proclaimed every commandment of the law to all the people, he took the blood of calves, together with water, scarlet wool and branches of hyssop, and sprinkled the scroll and all the people. He said, "This is the blood of the covenant, which God has commanded you to keep." In the same way, he sprinkled with the blood both the tabernacle and everything used in its ceremonies. In fact, the law requires that nearly everything be cleansed with blood, and without the shedding of blood there is no forgiveness (Hebrews 9:19-22).

Notice that last verse: "Without the shedding of blood, there is no forgiveness." If you mark your Bibles, you need to mark this important verse.

According to this verse, how much forgiveness is there without the shedding of blood? There is *no forgiveness*. So, for any Christian who thinks he needs *more* forgiveness for his sins than Jesus has already provided at the cross, what would have to happen? Jesus would have to die again. Is He going to do that? No, of course not. And that ought to tell us something about this new covenant of grace—that it's not only new, but it's also "a better covenant."

A Better Covenant

In Hebrews 8:6 we read, "But the ministry Jesus has received is as superior to theirs [that of the Old Testament high priests] as the covenant of which he is mediator is superior to the old one, and it is founded on better promises."

So Jesus' ministry as the high priest is as superior to that of the Old Testament priests as the new covenant is superior to the old covenant. Further, it says that this new covenant is founded on better promises.

> For if there had been nothing wrong with that first covenant, no place would have been sought for another. But God found fault with the people and said: "The time is coming, declares the Lord, when I will make a new covenant with the house of Israel and with the house of Judah. It will not be like the covenant I made with their forefathers when I took them by the hand to lead

them out of Egypt, because they did not remain
faithful to my covenant, and I turned away from
them, declares the Lord" (Hebrews 8:7-9).

Note that in verse 8 God doesn't say He found fault
with the covenant, but *with the people.* God's law is perfect. There's nothing in it that causes us to fall short. As
someone once said, "It's not the apple on the tree that's
the problem, but the pair on the ground." The problem
is you and me.

The Jews tried their very best to keep the law, but
failed miserably. If the Jews couldn't keep the law, why
do we think we can?

Now, some people will read these verses and say,
"That covenant is for Israel and the house of Judah. What
does it have to do with us?"

Let's use an illustration to demonstrate how it relates
to us. Picture before you, side by side, a Jewish man
dressed in tattered clothes and a Gentile man standing
there naked. God gave the law to the Jews to put on and
obey; the Gentile had nothing on. At Christ's death, the
new covenant was ushered in for both Jew and Gentile.

If we see the new covenant as a suit of new clothes to
be given to the Jew, what would I tell him to do with
what he was wearing? I would tell him to take it off and
put on the new, wouldn't I?

What would I tell the naked Gentile to do? I would
tell him to put on the new. Those of us who are Gentiles
were never under the law. We just put ourselves under it.

So the message of the new covenant from God to
the Jew was to take off the old, tattered rags of self-
righteousness brought about by their futile attempts to
obey the law, and to put on the new clothes of God's

grace and imputed righteousness, which is by faith. To the Gentile He said to simply put on the new.

The righteousness of the new covenant which comes through faith, a gift from God imputed to us, is new to the Gentile who never had a covenant with God. It is also new to the Jew, who had tried so hard to please God under the old covenant.

But what did those of us who are Gentiles do? We went over to Israel and took their old clothes of the law, which God told them to take off, and we put them on over our new suit of grace, and we walk around saying to ourselves, "Looking good." God never intended for Gentiles to put themselves under the law. In our fervor, wanting to please God through self-effort, we put ourselves under the law.

The Scriptures say in Hebrews 8:10-13:

> This is the [new] covenant I will make with the house of Israel after that time, declares the Lord. I will put my laws in their minds and write them on their hearts. I will be their God, and they will be my people. No longer will a man teach his neighbor, or a man his brother, saying, "Know the Lord," because they will all know me, from the least of them to the greatest. For I will forgive their wickedness and will remember their sins no more. By calling this covenant "new," he has made the first one obsolete; and what is obsolete and aging will soon disappear.

Notice the writer of Hebrews says God will put His laws in our minds and write them on our hearts. This is the only place where the Hebrew or Greek word for *law* is translated *laws*, plural. Why? Because, it's not talking about the law of Moses and the Ten Commandments, but about the laws of Jesus, which are: " 'Love the Lord your God with all your heart and with all your soul and with all your strength and with all your mind'; and, 'Love your neighbor as yourself'" (Luke 10:27).

He also ends this passage by saying, "Look, you have the old covenant that's obsolete and, if you let it age, it'll soon disappear."

He says the same thing to those of us who are Gentiles and have allowed ourselves to get under the law. We cannot be led by the law and the Spirit of God at the same time.

If you've been taught all of your life that the way to get forgiveness is by going to a confession booth or responding to an altar call, don't expect that habit to disappear overnight. As you put your roots deeply into Him and grow in your understanding of what Christ accomplished for you on the cross, you'll realize that there's no longer any meaning to those rituals. You will soon be asking, "Why am I walking down this church aisle to get my sins forgiven all over again?" "Why am I going back to the confession booth?" "Why am I constantly asking for what I already have? Could it be unbelief in what God said is finished?"

When we see Christ's finished work, we can rest in the fact that Jesus died for all our sins once and for all. There is nothing left for us to improve on, or any way to get new, additional forgiveness.

Hebrews 7:18,19 says, "The former regulation [covenant] is set aside because it was weak and useless (for the law made nothing perfect), and a better hope is introduced, by which we draw near to God." Why was it weak and useless? Because the law made nothing perfect, and a better hope was introduced by which we are able to draw near to God.

What was wrong with the old covenant? It could never make us perfect or complete. There were continuous sins that had to be dealt with by the repeated offering of animal sacrifices. How can we be complete or rest when we have to keep doing something to be forgiven?

The reason we can live by faith and know that we are complete and perfect under the new covenant is the superiority of the sacrifice of Christ compared to the blood of bulls and goats. Hebrews 10:1 says, "The law is only a shadow of the good things that are coming—not the realities themselves."

The observance of the law pointed to a time when our sins would be paid in full and the debt would be taken away forever. But as this verse says, those things in the law were only a shadow; they had no substance. There was no rest in the forgiveness provided through the law. How could there be when you had to keep getting forgiven over and over and over again? Rest and stability come when you realize and stand firm in the truth that you're forgiven *forever*.

> For this reason it can never, by the same sacrifices repeated endlessly year after year, make perfect those who draw near to worship. If it could, would they not have stopped being offered? For the worshipers would have been cleansed once for all, and would no longer have felt guilty for their sins. But those sacrifices are an annual reminder of sins, because it is impossible for the blood of bulls and goats to take away sins (Hebrews 10:1-4).

Under the old system, no one was cleansed once and for all. The animal sacrifices were not sufficient, nor worthy enough, to take away the sins of the people and to make them perfect and complete. If they were able to do so, they would have only been offered once, and the people would have stopped feeling guilty for their sins. But they were offered year after year. These sacrifices could never take away sins, only cover them. They just served as an annual reminder of sin, of the fact that the debt of punishment still needed to be paid. That punishment was death.

The blood of bulls and goats only *covered* sins, which is called "atonement." But Jesus didn't come to *atone* for sins. He came to take them away once and for all. Unfortunately, we've dragged the word *atonement* into the new covenant, even though you can't find it in the New Testament. If you see that word in your New Testament, in some versions you'll also find a footnote, with a clarification saying something like, "He is the one who turns aside God's wrath, taking away our sins."

I was reading a commentary one day on this subject that said, "Through continued theological usage the word 'atonement' has become an acceptable translation." That's a sad state of affairs, whereby continual theological usage becomes the standard for biblical interpretation. The reason the original Greek doesn't say *atonement* is that Jesus didn't come to atone for sin. He came to take sins away forever where they will never be seen again. "As far as the east is from the west, so far has he removed our transgressions from us" (Psalm 103:12).

> Therefore, when Christ came into the world, he
> said: "Sacrifice and offering you did not desire,

but a body you prepared for me; with burnt offerings and sin offerings you were not pleased. Then I said, 'Here I am—it is written about me in the scroll—I have come to do your will, O God.'" First he said, "Sacrifices and offerings, burnt offerings and sin offerings you did not desire, nor were you pleased with them" (although the law required them to be made). Then he said, "Here I am, I have come to do your will." He sets aside the first to establish the second. And by that will, *we have been made holy through the sacrifice of the body of Jesus Christ once for all* (Hebrews 10:5-10, emphasis added).

Do you know that through the sacrifice of Jesus Christ, God has made you holy in His sight? He did it once—and for how long? *Forever*. And if Jesus has made you holy forever, how much sense does it make for you to try to make yourself more holy? And when you're trying to make yourself more holy than Jesus made you, what are you saying to Jesus? You're telling Him, "You didn't do Your job very well, Jesus. There is something lacking in Your sacrifice on the cross.

Day after day every priest stands and performs his religious duties; again and again he offers the same sacrifices, which can never take away sins. But when this priest had offered for all time one sacrifice for sins, he sat down at the right hand of God. Since that time he waits for his enemies to be made his footstool, because by one sacrifice he has made perfect forever those who are being made holy (Hebrews 10:11-14).

Could the law make you perfect? No, it couldn't make anyone perfect. So what did God do? He provided the perfect lamb so that through His sacrifice on the cross He could make everyone perfect and complete through faith in Him.

In Christ Jesus, you have been made complete. Can you add to God's completeness? Can you take away from God's completeness? Are you ever going to get any more complete or any less complete?

When Jesus was on earth He told the people, "Be holy." He told them to be as holy as their Father in heaven. That's the only kind of holiness acceptable to God. On another occasion Jesus said, "Be perfect." How perfect? As perfect as your Father in heaven—that's all that will do.

When we read the commands of God, we're totally incapable of living up to them. And Jesus knew that no one can make himself holy and perfect, no matter how long or how much he may try. So what did Jesus do for us? By His one offering, He made us holy and perfect forever.

He made you and me as holy and perfect as our Father in heaven. He's declared us acceptable in His sight, and the only thing we can do is rest in this truth and give Him all the honor and glory.

> It was necessary, then, for the copies of the heavenly things to be purified with these sacrifices, but the heavenly things themselves with better sacrifices than these. For Christ did not enter a man-made sanctuary that was only a copy of the true one; He entered heaven itself, now to appear for us in God's presence. Nor did He

> enter heaven to offer Himself again and again,
> the way the high priest enters the Most Holy
> Place every year with blood that is not his own.
> Then Christ would have had to suffer many
> times since the creation of the world (Hebrews
> 9:23-26).

If there was any further forgiveness to be executed on our behalf, what would Jesus have to do? Obviously He would have to come and die again, for "without the shedding of blood there is no forgiveness." The writer of Hebrews is saying here that if Jesus' sacrifice was like that of bulls and goats, He would have to suffer over and over again. But no, the Scripture declares that He "appeared once for all at the end of the ages to do away with sin by the sacrifice of himself" (Hebrews 9:26).

Did sin need to be dealt with? Yes. How did God deal with it under the old covenant? Every year the people had to go through the Day of Atonement. They dealt with sin over and over and over again. How does He deal with sin in the new covenant? Christ died once for all. He did it all—complete, final! He came to do away with sin forever by the one sacrifice of Himself. He was the only perfect One worthy to deal with sin. "Just as man is destined to die once, and after that to face judgment, so Christ was sacrificed once to take away the sins of many people; and He will appear a second time, not to bear sin, but to bring salvation to those who are waiting for Him" (Hebrews 9:27,28).

This new covenant, simply put, is that Christ has taken away the sins of the world *forever*. In the Old Testament, atonement *covered* sins. In the New Testament, Christ *removed* them. John the Baptist said, "Look, the

Lamb of God who takes away the sin of the world" (John 1:29). Then in Hebrews 1:3, we read, "After He had provided purification for sins, He sat down at the right hand of the Majesty in heaven."

Why did He sit down? Because His work was completed.

> Day after day every priest stands and performs his religious duties; again and again he offers the same sacrifices, which can never take away sins. But when this priest [Jesus] had offered for all time one sacrifice for sins, He sat down at the right hand of God (Hebrews 10:11,12).

The priests under the old covenant could never sit down because their work was never finished. As a matter of fact, a chair was a prohibited piece of furniture in the temple. The sacrifices the priests offered only covered past sins. Jesus' sacrifice however, dealt with sin for all time—going back to Adam and forward to eternity. That's why He cried out from the cross, "It is finished" (John 19:30). God's not dealing with the world's sin anymore. The sin issue has been dealt with.

When people tell me, "But, Bob, I still sin," I ask them, "And what did Jesus do with those sins? He put them behind His back never to see them again."

According to Hebrews 10:17,18, He says, "Their sins and lawless acts I will remember no more." And where these have been forgiven, there is no longer any sacrifice for sin."

Some people say that this teaching on eternal forgiveness will give people a license to sin. But most people I know, including myself, don't need a license to sin. I sin quite well without a license. And so do you.

A radio personality once accused me of "circular reasoning." My reply to him is that I would rather be engaged in circular reasoning, whatever that means, than no reasoning at all. There is no logical reason for anyone to say, "Jesus did it all," and then ask Him to do something He has already done. "A double-minded man [is] unstable in all he does" (James 1:8) and is one who has never been reconciled to God. Saved—yes. Reconciled—no.

The idea that teaching people about their total forgiveness in Christ leads to a sinful lifestyle is an insult to the indwelling Christ who leads and directs a believer. Now if someone is void of the Spirit of God, he does not belong to God and is merely a religious person trying to be a Christian. But if Christ lives in you, why would He lead you to a license to sin? Why would asking God to forgive you every time you sin keep you from sinning? To me it seems to encourage sinning. Some people might reason this way: "After all, when I sin all I have to do is ask for forgiveness and the slate is clean." On the other hand, if you know you are a forgiven person, the only thing you can do is thank Him and enter into His presence and call Him "Daddy, Father," and receive mercy in the time of need. We have no fear of condemnation and no fear of coming into His presence for instruction and the renewing of our minds.

Have the sins that we will commit today or tomorrow been dealt with? Yes, totally. *All* our sin was dealt with once and for all at the cross. I can stand firm and rejoice in this fact and spend the rest of my life thanking Him for His total forgiveness.

A Forgiven Person

We've seen that Jesus' work on the cross ended the old way of God's dealing with sins through the annual animal sacrifice which "could never take away sins." We've seen that we've entered into a new covenant with God wherein all our sins—past, present, and future—are forever forgiven. Let's take some time to see exactly what this truth means.

If I could ask a group of assembled Christians to answer in unison the question, "How many of you believe Jesus said, 'It is finished'?" every hand would go up. If I then asked, "How many of you believe He *meant* 'It is finished,'?" we would get some Amens and Hallelujahs. But then if I asked, "How many of you are still asking God to forgive you?" we would still have people raising their hands all over the place. And I would have to tell them, "You have never put faith in what you say you believe. Because if you really had put faith in the fact that 'It is finished,' your hand wouldn't be raised."

Isn't it strange to think that a person's sins have been dealt with for 2,000 years, and yet he is still trying to get God to forgive him? When Jesus declared, "It is finished," I want to think that He *meant* it. How about you? What impact do those words have on your life? What kind of a person are you as a result of those words? Are you a person capable of receiving forgiveness, or are you a forgiven person?

I hope you answered that you're a *forgiven* person. The divine debt for our sins is paid for—finished! So what does faith say to this fact? Does it beg, "Oh, God, please forgive me!" Or does it say, "Oh, Lord, thank You that I am forever forgiven in Your sight because of Jesus!"

The problem with many Christians is that they mis-understand what forgiveness is. They haven't thought through what the book of Hebrews is clearly communi-cating concerning the sacrifice of Christ. They think that forgiveness of sins is doled out to the Christian on an "as needed" basis. It could be put to music: "Count your sins, name them one by one." When they sin, they think they need to ask to get forgiven for that sin. And they think that the next time they sin gains them a new expe-rience of forgiveness.

Paul tells us, "In Him we have redemption through his blood, the forgiveness of sins, in accordance with the riches of God's grace" (Ephesians 1:7). According to this verse, if you are in Christ, you *have* redemption. In other words, you *are* a redeemed person. Because of this truth, would it make sense to ask God to redeem you every day? That wouldn't be faith. In the same way, it doesn't make sense to continue to ask God for more forgiveness. You are a forgiven person. Rest in it. Believe that as far as your sins are concerned, "It is finished!"

When I first realized this tremendous truth, I can't describe the sense of rest that came into my heart. The completeness of my salvation overwhelmed me. It still does every day. I ask, "Who am I that You should be mindful of me?"

Forgiveness of sin is no longer a doctrine; it's life itself. In God's eyes, my forgiveness and redemption are absolute, not relative facts. And so are yours. And God wants us to rest in what is finished by Him.

Christ Jesus has done it all. Yet we forget to rest in His provision. We forget and we fall back into self-effort. Our habit of asking for more forgiveness, more redemption, more righteousness, and more sanctification must be replaced with a habit of trusting Him. He has done everything for us. And living by faith in what He has done for us is what pleases Him.

To help you understand God's wonderful provision for forgiveness of sin, take a look at the chart on page 98. This diagram illustrates the three possibilities for forgiveness of sin that mankind embraces. The first option lists the fate of those with no forgiveness. They go through life as unforgiven people, with no hope and no recourse but to "eat, drink, and be merry." The second option is the one under which most Christians mistakenly operate. They believe their faith in Christ grants them only partial, conditional forgiveness. They see themselves as having the *potential* to be forgiven—if they fulfill the right conditions.

The third option, however, illustrates the Christian's real situation. He has *total*, unconditional forgiveness and is, in fact, a forgiven person. There is nothing for the Christian to do then but to rejoice and thank God for His provision for sin, and live daily with that thankful attitude.

If you've never stopped to ponder how great your salvation is, I want you to take a few moments before you move on to the next chapter and thank God for *your* complete, finished, and perfect salvation. You are loved and accepted unconditionally by God.

Because we are His forgiven children, new creatures in Christ, the writer of Hebrews goes on to say, "Therefore, brothers, since we have confidence to enter the Most Holy Place by the blood of Jesus, by a new and living way opened for us through the curtain, that is, his body, and since we have a great priest over the house of God, let us

God's Provision for Forgiveness of Sin

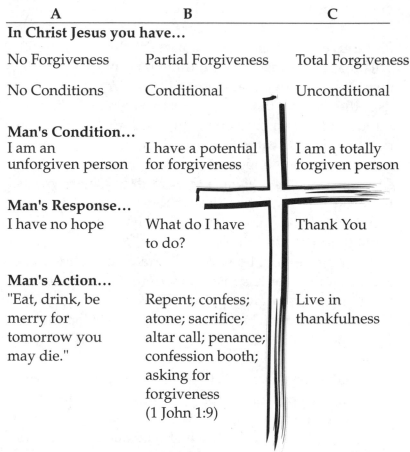

A	B	C
In Christ Jesus you have...		
No Forgiveness	Partial Forgiveness	Total Forgiveness
No Conditions	Conditional	Unconditional
Man's Condition...		
I am an unforgiven person	I have a potential for forgiveness	I am a totally forgiven person
Man's Response...		
I have no hope	What do I have to do?	Thank You
Man's Action...		
"Eat, drink, be merry for tomorrow you may die."	Repent; confess; atone; sacrifice; altar call; penance; confession booth; asking for forgiveness (1 John 1:9)	Live in thankfulness

draw near to God with a sincere heart in full assurance of faith" (Hebrews 10:19-22).

God wants us to be stable and to have our roots deeply planted in Him. Our "full assurance of faith" makes us confident and secure because He is faithful. We're reminded of this in Hebrews 4:16, which encourages us to "approach the throne of grace with confidence, so that we may receive mercy and find grace to help us in our time of need."

As forgiven people, we are partakers of God's new covenant. We go into God's presence not by concentrating on cleaning ourselves up beforehand, or with false humility, but *with confidence.* Why can we do this? Because by faith in Him we have been made complete. There's nothing to keep us from entering into God's presence with full assurance of faith.

When I think of this great access to the throne of God that is ours, I'm reminded of the famous snapshot published in *Life* magazine of John Kennedy Jr. when he was just a toddler, playing under his father's desk in the Oval Office. This was during the Cuban missile crisis when the threat of nuclear war hung in the balance. President Kennedy and several of his advisers were standing in a tight cluster discussing how to diffuse the threat—and yet, we catch a glimpse of a small boy crawling on the floor through his father's legs. He bypassed security guards, secretaries, and even the chief of staff in order to be in his father's presence. And when he entered the room, he had no cares, no worries. His daddy was in charge. He knew he was secure when he was with his father.

This is a wonderful picture of what our relationship with God can and should be. You and I are children of God. Matthew tells us that at the moment Christ gave up His spirit on the cross, "the curtain of the temple was torn in two from top to bottom" (Matthew 27:51). The doors are wide open. You have free access to God. You can enter into His presence at any time, and do so boldly, *because He loves you.*

Stop roaming in the desert. Enter into the promised land of rest. Rest from your works just as He rested from His. Rather than reaching up to God for His acceptance, receive the acceptance you already have in Christ Jesus.

The event that happened on Calvary 2,000 years ago requires a response from every person. In light of what Christ accomplished, the right response—the only response—is to rest securely in the finished work of the cross and give thanks. This is the response that pleases God, a response of faith.

There is nothing we can add to what Christ has done. The debt for sin has been paid in full. The work is finished. Because of His death, we live under the new covenant where He remembers our sins and lawless deeds no more. Rejoice and be grateful. This is good news.

And friend, until you can rest in the finality of the cross, you will never rest in the reality of the resurrection.

Hindrances to a Proper Response to Total Forgiveness

In the "Classic Christianity" conference that I teach nationwide, I spend well over four hours laying out Scriptures that point to the completeness of our forgiveness and our right standing before God. These are imputed to us, not because of our efforts, but because of the finished work of Jesus. I first establish the fact that we live under the new covenant and not the old. Then I read verse after verse which tell in the clearest of terms that we have been forgiven of all our sins—past, present, and future. I include verses such as

> When you were dead in your sins and in the
> uncircumcision of your sinful nature, God made
> you alive with Christ. He forgave us all our sins,
> having canceled the written code, with its regu-
> lations, that was against us, and that stood
> opposed to us; he took it away, nailing it to the
> cross (Colossians 2:13,14).

> I am sending you to them to open their eyes and turn them from darkness to light, and from the power of Satan to God, so that they may receive forgiveness of sins and a place among those who are sanctified by faith in Me (Acts 26:17,18).

> All the prophets testify about Him that everyone who believes in Him receives forgiveness of sins through His name (Acts 10:43).

> I write to you, dear children, because your sins have been forgiven on account of His name (1 John 2:12).

> All this is from God, who reconciled us to Himself through Christ and gave us the ministry of reconciliation: that God was reconciling the world to Himself in Christ, not counting men's sins against them (2 Corinthians 5:18,19).

The message of our complete forgiveness in Christ is so clear. Yet invariably, after all those hours of teaching, someone raises his hand to ask, "What about 1 John 1:9?" For many believers this is the only verse they have memorized that deals with forgiveness. The verse reads, "If we confess our sins, He is faithful and just and will forgive us our sins and purify us from all unrighteousness." Many believers read this and conclude that forgiveness is based on confession. If we confess, He forgives. If we don't confess, He won't forgive.

From a human perspective this sounds good, but is there still more forgiveness to be received for the already-forgiven Christian? No, there isn't. However, many Christian teachers have read that verse and camped on it for support of their predetermined opinion as to what the Christian response to personal sin should be. I liken this to something I've observed at professional football games.

I'm a big fan of the Dallas Cowboys and am always eager to see them win. But I get amused when a referee calls a play against the Cowboys. Fans sitting in the upper deck boo and hiss at the ref's "bad call." From hundreds of feet away, they're sure that what they saw was different than what the ref on the field saw—surely the ref must have looked away for a moment. In reality, they observed the play through prejudiced eyes. Having arrived at the conclusion they want, they can't be bothered with the facts. Many Christians act the same way when it comes to the explanation of 1 John 1:9; in fact, they can get pretty mad.

We must remember that if we start with a false premise, then our findings will be wrong—perhaps even dangerous. For example, if we go to a doctor and he misdiagnoses our illness as being tuberculosis and prescribes the wrong medicine, we may die or develop other illnesses from taking the wrong drug.

So when a person hears all the other passages concerning the totality of our forgiveness, confusion arises upon reading 1 John 1:9, which seems to make forgiveness dependent on confession. How can you say on one hand that you are totally forgiven, and then turn around and say you need to confess your sins to receive forgiveness? Just the fact the question comes up should raise a red flag. I believe that through an improper understanding of what this verse really means, we have negated the power of the cross of Jesus Christ.

I can understand the confusion. Two weeks after I came to Christ, I was taught a concept called "spiritual breathing." This is a spiritual exercise that calls for the believer to confess to God any known sin at the moment he becomes aware of it. After confessing, the believer is then urged to claim and appropriate God's forgiveness for that sin. That is the "exhaling" part. He then appropriates the power of the Holy Spirit by claiming that he is filled by faith. That is the "inhaling" part.

When I was first taught the concept of spiritual breathing, I asked the person who taught me why we had to ask to be forgiven, when all our sins were already forgiven at the cross. I was told, "We do this to make real in our own experience what God has already provided."

That answer never really made sense to me, but I was a new Christian, and at least I had a response when other people asked me about the practice of spiritual breathing. And when others asked, I repeated like a parrot the same answer I had been given. I felt that if someone would push my belly button, out would come, "To make real in our own experience what God's already provided."

My problem was that after about a year, my spiritual breathing turned to spiritual panting. After three years I was spiritually hyperventilating. It just didn't work.

For all my good intentions, I had grown weary and tired, and I noticed the misapplication of 1 John 1:9 led to a serious problem in my thinking. My concentration was on sin. My whole focus turned away from Jesus to a preoccupation with sin and how to get rid of it. I had, as someone once said, an obsession with confession. In that state of mind I had no time to focus on what Christ had accomplished for me at the cross. And the more a person thinks about sin, the more he sows to the sinful flesh. Instead of resting in the truth that *all* our sins have been dealt with at Calvary, we still keep riding the bicycle of forgiveness, wearing ourselves out. We act no different than the Old Testament Jew who went back to Jerusalem year after year to offer the blood of bulls and goats to cover the sins committed the previous year.

Any good theologian will tell you that it's intellectual suicide to build an entire doctrine around one verse of Scripture. But that's exactly what we have done with 1 John 1:9. Nowhere in the New Testament, after the crucifixion, is the concept of asking God's forgiveness even mentioned. The apostle Paul never broached the subject—he didn't have to. He stood firm in the fact that he was a forgiven person and that those to whom he wrote were forgiven people.

When God took away our sins, He took all of them. He bought us, knowing our past, present, and future. Jesus paid the debt *in full*. Now, in Him, we have redemption, the forgiveness of sins.

> For he has rescued us from the dominion of darkness and brought us into the kingdom of the Son He loves, in whom we have redemption, the forgiveness of sins (Colossians 1:13,14).
>
> In Him we have redemption through His blood, the forgiveness of sins, in accordance with the riches of God's grace (Ephesians 1:7).

Repeatedly, I am asked about 1 John 1:9 because this erroneous application of the verse is so widely taught and accepted today. And yet, this one reference in the book of 1 John is the only time this concept is mentioned in the New Testament. This should be a red flag to any thinking student of the Bible.

Although "spiritual breathing" was the way I was taught to apply 1 John 1:9, others have used terms such as "judicial" and "parental" forgiveness to explain how 1 John 1:9 should be used to obtain forgiveness. One day a Dallas Theological Seminary student called to inform me that this was "forensic" forgiveness. I told him, "Good gracious, now you have 'Quincy' involved in this thing."

People will say, "Now, if my child goes out and does something wrong, he needs to come to me and ask forgiveness." In other words, rather than elevating our thoughts to God's form of forgiveness, we pull God down to our way of thinking about forgiveness. Incidentally, all of these theories are in direct opposition to the overwhelming evidence of the New Testament that our sins *have been forgiven forever* and there is no more sacrifice for sins.

Many Christians may not know what the Bible teaches concerning forgiveness; however, when they sin, they confess to God and ask for His forgiveness according to 1 John 1:9 simply out of tradition. Though these believers are well meaning, ultimately the misapplication of this verse works *against* their understanding of the forgiveness of sins, and thus results in continually working in vain for something they already have.

One day as I was pondering this widespread error, I thought about what it would have been like for Christ to be hanging on the cross, enduring the torture and punishment for our sins, finally crying out in pain, "Father, forgive them for they know not what they do." And there at the foot of the cross is standing one of these 1 John 1:9 theologians who looks up at Christ and asks,

"Jesus, are You talking about judicial or parental forgiveness?"

In and Out of Fellowship

Another problem connected to this erroneous teaching is the idea that a Christian can fall in and out of fellowship with God. It creates anxiety when we're taught that every time we sin we're out of fellowship until we confess that sin and clear our account with God. The problem with this theory is that you can't find it in the Bible. You are either in the fellowship and saved, or out of the fellowship and lost. Period. "Fellowship" is two fellows in the same ship. Those who hold to this theology and say that the result of their sin is falling out of fellowship with God are totally watering down the truth that the wages of sin is *death*. They're also watering down the gift of God, which is life—the resurrected life of Jesus. The Bible says the punishment for sin is death, not being out of fellowship. In the same way, His gift of grace is eternal life, not being "in fellowship."

The assumption of those who promote this "in and out of fellowship" teaching of 1 John 1:9 is that their confession brings about forgiveness. We *initiate* to God through confession; He *responds* to us with forgiveness. Once again we put God in the position of being the responder and us the initiators. But remember, from God's point of view there is no forgiveness without the shedding of blood. He did that once for all at the cross. He initiated; we respond.

Neither our faith nor our confession of sin creates forgiveness. Our faith accesses the forgiveness that's already been provided. If every Christian would have the attitude that he or she is forever a forgiven person, what tremendous freedom he or she would experience from unnecessary guilt and from sin itself.

Whom Is 1 John 1:9 Addressing?

Obviously, 1 John 1:9 has great meaning. All of Scripture is "God-breathed and is useful for teaching, rebuking, correcting and training in righteousness" (2 Timothy 3:16). So the true meaning of 1 John 1:9 and to whom he was speaking is important if we're going to understand this verse.

You will hear it said that all Scripture is written only to believers. This is utter nonsense. If that were the case, every church that was planning to teach out of the Bible should have a salvation check at the front door. When Paul and Peter penned their letters, they were writing to a Christian pastor who was to read the letter to a congregation made up of both lost and saved people, just like the congregations of today. The saved are built up in their faith, and the lost have the opportunity to see their need for salvation and come to faith in Jesus Christ.

Reading 1 John in context, we see that it's addressing the lost, not the believer. At the time John wrote this letter, about A.D. 90, a heretical group known as the Gnostics had infiltrated the Christian assemblies. The Gnostics believed that all matter is evil, that only spirit is good. Therefore, Jesus couldn't have come in the flesh, because flesh is matter. So they concluded that Jesus was an illusion.

Today we still find these doctrines taught through such groups as the Christian Scientists and other metaphysical "churches."

John was thus addressing this issue in his first letter. Notice how it begins: "That which was from the beginning, which we have heard, which we have seen with our own eyes, which we have looked at and our hands have touched—this we proclaim concerning the Word of life" (1 John 1:1).

Why do you suppose John begins his letter this way? It was to dispel this Gnostic heresy that was making the rounds in the churches in those days.

This error is illustrated in a story of a boy who came home one day and said to his modern-Gnostic mother, "Hey, Mom, did you know that our neighbor Mr. Jones is sick?"

His mom replied, "Oh no, son, he's not sick. He just thinks he's sick."

The next day the boy came in from playing and again said, "Mom, Mr. Jones is really sick today."

"No, no," she replied. "He just thinks he's sick."

The following day the boy came in the house and called out, "Hey, Mom, today Mr. Jones thinks he's dead."

Now, let me ask you, if Jesus did not come in the flesh, what does that do to the gospel message? If He did not die physically, we are still under condemnation of sin and death. If He was not raised physically, we are still spiritually dead, separated from the life of Christ. So to deny that Jesus came in the flesh is to deny the gospel.

One other paramount teaching of the Gnostics was that man didn't have a sin nature. And even if he did, it didn't matter. John addresses this heresy in verses 8 and 10 of 1 John 1. We quote 1 John 1:9 so often that we seldom look at what is said in the verses before and after: "If we claim to be without sin, we deceive ourselves and the truth is not in us....If we claim we have not sinned, we make him out to be a liar and his word has no place in our lives" (1 John 1:8,10).

To help clarify that this is a passage to unbelievers, John wrote in his second letter, "To the chosen lady and her children, whom I love in the truth—and not I only, but also all who know the truth—because of the truth which lives in us and will be with us forever" (2 John 1,2). Compare this with 1 John 1:8, which says, "If we claim to be without sin, we deceive ourselves and the truth is not in us." If the truth lives in us and will be with us forever, then can a believer ever say that the truth is not in him? This would be double-talk. In one verse he says that if we claim to be without sin, the truth isn't in us. And yet later he says the truth lives in us and will be with us forever. How can these two verses both be referring to a Christian? The only conclusion we can make is that those in 1 John 1:8, who claim to be without sin, are lost and are later referred to as antichrists.

Several years ago I wanted to make sure I was reading this verse correctly, so I called one of the foremost Greek language professors at the renowned Dallas Theological Seminary. I made an appointment and met with Dr. John Best. During our discussion he told me that for years he had accepted as truth the common explanation of 1 John 1:9—that it's written to the Christian. But then he told me that he recently had investigated deeper, examining the book of 1 John without considering the preconceived doctrines he had long held to. The result of his study, he maintained, was that 1 John 1:9 *must* be referring to an unbeliever. Of that he was now certain.

Dr. Best interprets the verse as follows. First of all, it is addressed to the lost Gnostics who claim to be without sin. To them the Apostle John states, "If we [an editorial we] claim to be without sin, we are deceiving ourselves and God's truth is not in us." Now for the "if." In 1 John 1:9, the phrase, "if we confess our sins," is classified as a third-class conditional clause, which means that the condition stated by the "if" clause is in question. The Apostle John was not sure whether or not the Gnostics would agree with God concerning their sins and turn to Him for salvation. The Greek structure of this passage forces the following interpretation: "I don't know if you are ever going to come to your senses or not and agree with God concerning your sins. But, if at anytime—today, tomorrow, or whenever—you should decide to turn to Him, God can be depended upon to have forgiven your sins and to have cleansed you of all unrighteousness." Notice the past tense.

So let me ask you: When is the only time you were forgiven of all your sins and cleansed of your unrighteousness?

It was at the cross.

When you first came to Christ and saw that 2,000 years ago He bore the totality of your sins, you received that once-and-for-all-time cleansing of your sins that took place on the cross.

First John 1:9 is a marvelous salvation passage we have mistakenly applied to the believer and called it the "Christian bar of soap" by which we can keep ourselves clean. The truth is the Christian doesn't need a bar of soap. He has already been cleansed once and forever by the blood of Christ. And we can rest in the fact and confidently say that God is not counting our sins against us. Paul affirms this in 2 Corinthians 5:19, where we're told that God was in Christ reconciling the world to Himself, *not counting men's sins against them.*

The entire New Testament deals with the completed work of the cross, and yet we, by taking one verse and misapplying it, negate the primary message of the whole New Testament. We rob the cross of Christ of its full power to save from sin.

Misunderstanding the Lord's Prayer

Another passage of Scripture we have misused is the Lord's Prayer. When Jesus' disciples asked how they should pray, Jesus told them not to do as the heathen, who take a prayer and pray it over and over again. Instead, He said, "This then, is how you should pray," and He gave an example of how to pray. And so what do we do? We take those guidelines, label them as "The Lord's Prayer," and, like the heathen, we pray that prayer over and over again!

There's nothing wrong with the prayer that Jesus prayed, but keep in mind you never read in Scripture of Paul, Peter, or anyone else praying or repeating those same words. It wasn't meant to be a rote prayer. It was to show His disciples *how* to pray.

It's important to remember that when Jesus was talking about this prayer to His disciples, they were still living under the old covenant—under the law. He hadn't yet gone to the cross to initiate the new covenant and was, in fact, still teaching under the old. Whenever we look at the teachings of Christ, we need to remember at what period of time He taught. It was before the cross. It was under the old covenant because the new didn't go into effect until Jesus died, fulfilling the old.

In His prayer, Jesus taught us to pray the words everyone remembers so well: "Forgive us our trespasses as we forgive those who trespass against us." Many people would say, "See, that shows that we need to ask God to forgive our sins." But please read on; the passage doesn't stop there. Jesus goes on to say, "For if you forgive men when they sin against you, your heavenly Father will also forgive you. But if you do not forgive men their sins, your Father will not forgive your sins" (Matthew 6:14,15).

Under the old covenant, forgiveness from God was conditional, based on our forgiveness of other people. But is this true after the cross, under the new covenant? Paul tells us in Colossians 3:13, "Bear with each other and forgive whatever grievances you may have against one another. *Forgive as the Lord forgave you.*"

Paul repeats this important truth on forgiveness in Ephesians 4:32: "Be kind and compassionate to one another, forgiving each other, just as in Christ God forgave you." Under the old covenant, a person forgave in order to receive forgiveness. Under the new, we forgive because we are forgiven—a new and different motivation of the heart altogether.

I know this is controversial and will arouse loud protests. When I first began to understand this, it seemed like double-talk—or worse yet, triple-talk! On the one hand, we're told that in Christ all our sins are forgiven, and yet on the other, Jesus says that we won't be forgiven unless we forgive others. Then in 1 John 1:9, we're told that we must continually be confessing our sins to be forgiven.

It didn't make sense to me that if, in God's sight, I'm clothed with the imputed righteousness of Christ and am standing not in my righteousness but His, why I would be asking Him to cleanse me of all unrighteousness?

Either I have the righteousness of Christ or I don't. It can't be both. I had to give Him my unrighteousness at the cross in order to take on His righteousness by faith. In Romans 3:21,22 Paul writes, "But now a righteousness from God, apart from law, has been made known, to which the Law and the Prophets testify. This righteousness from God comes through faith in Jesus Christ to all who believe."

Some earnest Christians who are steeped in the concept of continually confessing and receiving fresh forgiveness for sin say that the result of not confessing and receiving new forgiveness is to demean God's grace. I say that continued asking for what we already have is unbelief and a mockery of God's grace.

When we grasp the immeasurable value of the payment for our sins—the death of the Son of God on the cross—we'll never look at God's grace as "cheap grace" or an open door to sinning or, like so many call it, "a license to sin." No, God didn't wink at or overlook our sins. He saw them all 2,000 years ago, and He saw the severity of our slavery to sin, and in His mercy He provided redemption. The punishment for every sin you or I have ever committed or ever will commit was meted out to Christ. He paid a debt He did not owe, for us who owed a debt we could not pay. To grasp this truth makes His death all the more precious and meaningful and the gospel all the more glorious. *No sin has gone unpunished.* He took it *all* on Himself. That's the measure of His love for us. His forgiveness of sins is total, eternal, and irreversible.

So then, the believer who sins doesn't need more forgiveness. He is a forgiven person. With a thankful heart to God, he or she needs to understand that the payment for that sin, as well as all past sins and all the future ones, was made once and for all on the cross. In realizing this amazing grace, the believer looks to God and sees His unconditional love, which makes him respond to God in overwhelming love and with a deep desire to sin no more. It is the grace of God that teaches us to say no to unrighteousness.

Please don't get me wrong concerning confession of sin. I'm not saying that a Christian shouldn't confess his sins. What I am saying is that confession doesn't bring about forgiveness. Only the blood of Christ can do that. We will talk more on what true biblical confession is in the next chapter, but right now let's agree with God concerning the marvelous fact that we are forgiven people because of the cross of Jesus Christ.

Misunderstanding the Book of Hebrews

Another hindrance to walking by faith in the totality of forgiveness is found in the misunderstanding of key passages in the book of Hebrews. Many Christians have agonized over their sins because they believed or maybe were taught that there is no more forgiveness available for them because of some awful act of sin they have committed.

One gentleman I talked with believed this because, when he was a teenager, he used the Lord's name in vain. For years he struggled with guilt and the thought that God could not forgive him. And his misunderstanding of the passages we are about to discuss kept him in bondage.

The first of these verses is

> It is impossible for those who have once been enlightened, who have tasted the heavenly gift, who have shared in the Holy Spirit, who have

tasted the goodness of the word of God and the powers of the coming age, if they fall away, to be brought back to repentance, because to their loss they are crucifying the Son of God all over again and subjecting him to public disgrace (Hebrews 6:4-6).

Many Christians get confused as to whom the writer is talking. He's referring to people who don't believe that Jesus' sacrifice was sufficient to take away all our sins. He's saying that since Christ died for all our sins, it's impossible to be brought back to repentance when it's obvious that you've never repented, or changed your mind, to begin with. You've never changed your mind about what Jesus did for you at Calvary. There are many people today in the same boat.

If I am asking God to forgive me as a saved person, what would He have to do to answer that prayer? He would have to die again. Why? Because without the shedding of blood there is no forgiveness. What would I be doing if I am asking Him to die for me again? I would be subjecting Him to public disgrace and crucifying the Son of God all over again. Why would I want Him to die again? Why would I want to see my Lord stripped naked and beaten? Why would I want to see Jesus suffer again so that I could "feel" forgiven? *To depend on feelings is a repudiation of faith.* I don't need to feel forgiven, I *am* forgiven, and I need to live by faith in that fact. So do you. For us to expect Christ to deal with sin again or to come back and be sacrificed all over is to grossly misunderstand the nature of what happened on the cross. It is an insult to the Lord Jesus.

The other passage in Hebrews is used by legalists to say that you can lose your salvation or that you can backslide. The reality is there is no backslider. There may be someone who has forgotten his total forgiveness and falls back to trust in his obedience to the law to gain God's favor. Again he becomes sin-focused, instead of walking by faith. For example, someone says, "I've backslidden. I've started sinning all over again." I've got news for that person: He never stopped sinning. Sin, in the Bible, is unbelief. That which is not of faith is sin. What was sin in the Garden of Eden? It surely wasn't adultery—there wasn't anyone there to commit it with. There was nothing to steal. No, the sin in the garden is the same sin that exists throughout the Bible: unbelief. The verse in question here is: "If we deliberately keep on sinning after we have received the knowledge of the truth, no sacrifice for sins is left, but only a fearful expectation of judgment and of raging fire that will consume the enemies of God" (Hebrews 10:26,27).

Friends, what it says here is that if we deliberately keep on sinning, living in unbelief after we've received the knowledge of the truth—the truth of the finality of the cross—there is no sacrifice for sins left. Sinning here doesn't mean committing adultery or stealing or coveting or what I call the "dirty dozen" or the "nasty nine." The sin the writer of Hebrews is discussing is the deliberate rejection and demeaning of the sacrifice of Christ. The writer was addressing his fellow kinsmen who had heard the truth, yet were continuing to depend on the old covenant ritual of the sacrificial system. To them the blood of bulls and goats was of equal value to the blood of Jesus.

If we reject the sacrifice of Christ, what other sacrifice is there? If Jesus' sacrifice wasn't sufficient or good enough, then there isn't anything or anyone else to do more. And if you don't accept His sacrifice for you as sufficient, all you have to look forward to is a fearful expectation of judgment and the raging fire.

Why? *Because you are lost.* Until you accept and rest in *His* sacrifice, you can't be saved.

> Anyone who rejected the law of Moses died without mercy on the testimony of two or three witnesses. How much more severely do you think a man deserves to be punished who has trampled the Son of God under foot, who has treated as an unholy thing the blood of the covenant that sanctified him, and who has insulted the Spirit of grace? (Hebrews 10:28,29).

What are you and I doing when we continually try to add to what Christ said is finished? We deny the finality of the cross. In our pride we are saying we can improve on Christ's work. When we refuse to walk by faith and in some way want to have something to do with our salvation, we are insulting the Spirit of grace. We're treating as an unholy thing the blood of the covenant that set us apart.

When the Israelite who hears that Christ's sacrifice has taken away his sin, yet continues to go to the Day of Atonement to offer animal sacrifices to atone for his sins, what is he saying about the blood of Christ? The Catholic who continues to rely on his priest for forgiveness, what is he saying about the Spirit of grace? The Protestant who continues to send up prayers of confession to bring about forgiveness, what is he saying about the blood of the covenant? The Christian world tells the Israelites, "You no longer have to offer animal sacrifices." The Protestants are saying to the Catholics, "You don't have to confess to a priest, you can go direct to God." And God in heaven is saying to *all* of us, "IT IS FINISHED."

Believe it. There is nothing more to do. Don't let a misunderstanding of these passages become a hindrance to your response to the finality of the cross.

In his classic book *Faith's Checkbook*, Charles Haddon Spurgeon, the great preacher of the nineteenth century, wrote these powerful words concerning Christ's sacrifice on the cross:

> According to this gracious covenant, the Lord treats His people as if they had never sinned. Practically, He forgets all their trespasses. Sins of all kinds He treats as if they had never been; as if they were quite erased from His memory. O miracle of grace! God here does that which in certain aspects is impossible to Him. His mercy works miracles which far transcends all other miracles. Our God ignores our sin now that the sacrifice of Jesus has ratified the covenant. We may rejoice in Him without fear that He will be provoked to anger against us because of our iniquities. See! He puts us among the children; He accepts us as righteous; He takes delight in us as if we were perfectly holy. He even puts us in places of trust; makes us guardians of His honor, trustees of the crown jewels, stewards of the gospel. He counts us worthy, and gives us a ministry; this is the highest and most special proof that He does not remember our sins. Even

when we forgive an enemy, we are very slow to trust him; we judge it to be imprudent to do so. But the Lord forgets our sins, and treats us as if we had never erred. O my soul, what a promise is this! Believe it and be happy.

I concur with him. Believe it and be happy.

What the Bible Says About Confession and Forgiveness

ONE AFTERNOON I RECEIVED a phone call from one of the students who ran the control board in the radio station we were on in New Orleans. The station was owned and operated by the local seminary, and the student was telling me that several local pastors were up in arms about my teaching on freewill giving versus tithing. Also in the mix was the finality of the cross. It seems that they had informed the president that if our program wasn't removed from the air, they were going to withdraw their support of the cooperative program and anything else needed to get this heretical teaching off the air.

Obviously, they had met in private and had discussed their plan of attack prior to this event. They had served as the judge and jury, and I had been declared guilty in their sight. I asked the student to get the names and addresses of the ones who had made the threat to the seminary and to send them to me. I then proceeded to write them a letter, explaining to them how the Bible states that if you have ought against a brother, to go to that brother and straighten out the problem. I further explained that, inasmuch as this was not done, I was coming to them with an invitation to meet with me on a certain day at one of the local hotels and discuss our areas of disagreement.

The day came and I, along with a number of laymen both from Dallas and New Orleans, arrived at the hotel and waited for the others to come. Finally, they all entered the prearranged meeting room looking as if they had just consumed a skunk for lunch. I don't mean to be disrespectful, but that's the only description I can think of to describe their faces. They looked mean, angry, and ready for battle. I thanked them for coming, and the meeting began.

It seemed that they really didn't wish to talk about the tithing issue, but rather the issue of forgiveness, and especially as it deals with 1 John 1:9. (I think they knew that they were going to have to dig deep to come up with any verse in the New Testament to prove the practice of tithing.) I went to Scripture to verify why I believed that when Jesus cried from the cross, "It is finished," He meant "It is finished." If there was any further forgiveness to be executed on our behalf, He would have to die again, for "without the shedding of blood there is no forgiveness [of sins]" (Hebrews 9:21).

To be real honest, I might as well have been speaking in Swahili for all the good it did. Their attitude was, "Don't confuse me with facts; my mind is already made up." Finally, in utter desperation, one of the pastors asked me, "Bob, what do you do then when you sin?" I said, "My dear brother, this is a general question that can only be answered in a general manner. But Jesus didn't deal in generalities, only in specifics. So He would ask you, 'What specific sin are you dealing with?' "

After a pause, he said, "The sin of not liking you."

I said, "Brother, I couldn't think of a better example of what I'm talking about. What good do you think it is going to do for you to send up your 1 John 1:9 to God for the sin of not liking me, your brother in Christ, and then walk out of this room still not liking me? Don't you see that you can confess without ever repenting, but it is impossible to repent without confessing? You are willing to talk to God, but not to me. You are willing to ask God to forgive you, but you aren't willing to ask me to forgive you for plotting behind my back and trying to destroy a ministry that God called into existence. This is the type of hypocrisy that never wants to repent but only to confess until the next time you do it again—and then confess again and then again and again. Hebrews 10:11,12 says, 'Day after day every priest stands and performs his religious duties; again and again he offers the same sacrifices, which can never take away sins. But when this priest, Christ, had offered for all time one sacrifice for sins, He sat down at the right hand of God.' Why did He sit down? Because His work was over! The issue isn't between you and God. That issue was settled 2,000 years ago. The issue is between you and me, and that issue needs to be settled today."

There was a strange and deafening silence in the room, until finally one of the leaders stood to his feet and declared, "This is the end of the meeting. You are going off the air!"

The fact that we are totally forgiven people doesn't mean that we don't agree with God when we have acted or thought in a way inconsistent with our new identity in Christ. All of those men's sins, as well as mine, have already been forgiven. But when other people have been hurt by our actions, we need to go to them and confess our wrongdoing to them and to make it right.

That's why the book of James says to "confess your sins to each other and pray for each other so that you may be healed." Had this occurred with the pastors, we could have left the room agreeing to disagree, but as brothers in Christ. The call for confession of sins in James 5:16 refers to sins committed between two people. God's forgiveness isn't in question here. It's talking about forgiveness between brothers in Christ! In other words, it is horizontal forgiveness, not vertical. The instruction of James is no different than the instruction of Paul in Colossians 3:13, when he urged his readers to "forgive as the Lord forgave you." Notice the past tense: "as the Lord *forgave* you." There is no question about God's forgiveness. It's a done deal! The issue is between us. God calls us to exercise forgiveness toward those who have harmed us or with whom we do not agree, and to seek forgiveness from those we have hurt.

Confession According to the Bible

I've been misquoted and misunderstood on this issue of confession of sin. Some critics have accused me of saying that I don't believe that confession of sin has a place in the life of a Christian. That's not true.

Where we differ is on the purpose of confession. As we have established, most Christians confess their sins to God in order to get forgiveness from God. But confession doesn't bring about forgiveness. The blood of Christ has done that for us. So then, what role does confession play in the life of a believer?

True biblical confession is a natural response to our faith in God's truth. It's as natural to the believer as breathing. True confession agrees with God not only concerning sin, but also with the truth that we *are* forgiven, not that we *will be* forgiven. Then it goes a step further and agrees with God concerning the proper attitudes and actions that need to be taken in order to "work out what has been worked in."

You see, true confession focuses our mind not on our failures, but back to the finished work of Christ on the cross, which leads to a thankful heart. From God's perspective, confession isn't meant to be a sporadic, mechanical response. Instead, it's to be a continual, dependent attitude pulsating through the life of every believer walking in truth.

When we learn to agree with God concerning forgiveness, our minds begin to see the totality of grace that God has for us in Christ Jesus. Understanding God's grace is what changes the way we live. It enables us to see people, circumstances, and things through His eyes and respond out of a heart of love not only for God but for people around us. Consider the words of the apostle Paul to Titus, his "true son in our common faith": "For the grace of God that brings salvation has appeared to all men. It teaches us to say "No" to ungodliness and worldly passions, and to live self-controlled, upright and godly lives in this present age" (Titus 2:11,12).

According to this passage, what teaches us to say no to ungodliness? Grace. This may surprise you. You may be thinking that if you teach too much of grace, you're just going to lead people to sin. As a matter of fact, if I took a survey and asked people what is needed to encourage upright living, most would answer that it's the law. Just give me a set of rules and regulations, a list of dos and don'ts, and I will live a life of victory. But the truth is, it doesn't work that way. We will never be able to say no to ungodliness through self-effort or obedience to the law. If we try, we're going to fail. Our flesh simply isn't strong enough to overcome the power of sin.

If your desire is to say no to "ungodliness and worldly passions," then the apostle Paul advises you to learn about God's grace. When we respond to God's grace and are led by the Holy Spirit, we're empowered to live the kind of life that glorifies God. But when we engage in self-effort and legalism in attempts to gain God's forgiveness through our own works, we are sure to stumble. What's more, our attempts to receive what we already have are actually displays of unbelief toward God.

To ask for forgiveness indicates that we don't really believe we are forgiven people. Friend, *there is nothing more that God is going to do about your sin.* Nothing! Christ isn't going to die for it again. He did that once and for all at the cross. At the cross every sin has met its ultimate judgment, and God is pleased with His Son's accomplishments.

What I've discovered is that many Christians will confess the same sin over and over. They don't seem to be able to rid themselves of that one besetting weakness. They don't even believe that, when they confess, God is faithful and just to forgive. I have met Christians who are still trying to get God to forgive sins they committed decades ago. They've pleaded with God; they've tried to please Him by rededicating themselves every time there is an altar call. And yet the day they accepted Christ as Savior, they received complete and total forgiveness.

If you remember what we said in chapter 4, you may see what happens when we fall into a routine of asking God to forgive our sin. Oblivious of truth, we slip back into leaning upon our own understanding and so become again the initiator to God instead of a responder to Him. But remember, God never meant for us to be the initiator. He created this world and He initiates everything. Our part is to respond. When we sin, our recourse is to respond to Him with an awareness and recognition of a glorious fact: He has put that sin behind His back never to see it again. If this truth does not create in us an overflowing, thankful heart, then we are dead.

But again someone will raise the objection that the result of this wonderful grace will be a license to keep on sinning. And truly, it is a license to someone who is lost and doesn't have the Holy Spirit living in him. The Scriptures say that if the Holy Spirit doesn't dwell in you, you don't belong to Him. But if Jesus lives in you, will He lead you into a lifestyle of sin?

Paul answers this in Romans 6:1,2: "What shall we say, then? Shall we go on sinning so that grace may increase? By no means! We died to sin; how can we live in it any longer?"

Grace doesn't encourage sin in the Christian. Would Jesus, who is full of grace and truth, encourage us to sin? Grace teaches us that we are no longer slaves to sin. We don't have to respond or give in to the temptations of the flesh, the world, or the devil. If a Christian desires to sin or live in unbelief, there's something wrong with his heart. The law always deals with outward behavior, not the heart. Grace deals with the heart, where everything starts when a person's heart is changed, the actions will follow suit. Grace is about freedom, not bondage.

So what *is* the remedy when we do something wrong? Again, we can go back to the Scriptures and see Paul addressing this issue in the book of Ephesians. In that assembly of believers, a Christian had been found stealing—one of the Old Testament's big Ten Commandments. Paul's counsel to the guilty person was to steal no longer, but to go to work "doing something useful with his own hands, that he may have something to share with those in need" (Ephesians 4:28).

In the tradition in which I lived as a Christian, we would have faulted the apostle Paul for not saying to the Ephesian offender, "Hey, you're out of fellowship, buddy. God can't use you. You need to get that black mark off your record. You need to exhale the sin and inhale God's forgiveness." But instead, Paul simply says to stop stealing and go to work.

He didn't tell the person who stole to confess the sin to God to get forgiveness, because the man was already forgiven. He didn't need to confess to get back into fellowship with God. Paul knew the offender was a believer and in God's fellowship and would remain so throughout eternity because of God's faithfulness. First Corinthians 1:9 tells us, "God, who has called you into fellowship with his Son Jesus Christ our Lord, is faithful."

What this person needed was his mind renewed with truth. He had believed a lie of Satan, who tempted him to steal. If God said He would supply all our needs according to His riches in glory, does it make any sense to steal from a neighbor? If God owns the cattle on a thousand hills, can we trust Him to meet our needs?

Paul addresses several other common issues in the same passage. For example, he says, "Therefore each of you must put off falsehood and speak truthfully to his neighbor, for we are all members of one body" (Ephesians 4:25). Obviously, there were people in the church at Ephesus who were not always honest. They were lying to one another.

How did Paul respond? Did he respond in condemnation? No! He reasoned with them and brought them back to truth. If we all belong to each other as members of the body of Christ, it doesn't make any sense to lie to each other. How practical. Just think about what would happen if the parts of our physical body started lying to each other. If the head lied to the hand about the runny nose, we would have a problem. So it only makes sense to speak the truth.

Paul also gives directives concerning anger, unwholesome talk, bitterness, rage, and slander. In all of these, he reasons with us in love, saying that as a child of God this is inconsistent with who we are in Christ. It's like the caterpillar and the butterfly. I have used this illustration before, but its application is so important that it is worth repeating here.

Initially, a caterpillar is a hairy, ugly, earthbound creature. You can try to change the caterpillar by dressing it up, making it smell nice, or even educate it at Worm University, but it's still a caterpillar. For the caterpillar to change, it must go through the process of metamorphosis.

When it does, the caterpillar weaves a cocoon and is totally immersed in it. Within the cocoon the process of metamorphosis takes place. Finally, a brand-new creature emerges called a butterfly. Once ground-bound, the butterfly can now soar through the sky.

In the same way, you and I came into this world as sinners, separated from the life of Christ. In this condition, we, too, try to look good, smell good, and educate ourselves to act good, but underneath we are still sinners. Then, through what the Bible calls new birth, we are made new. When we place our faith in Jesus Christ, we pass from death to life and emerge as brand-new creatures with Christ living in us.

As new creatures in Christ, we may not always act like new creations. Sometimes we forget we're butterflies and go back and do worm things, like crawl around with all our worm buddies. When we sin today, we can imagine God holding up a heavenly mirror and saying, "Look up here."

"Okay, Lord."

"What do you see?"

"I see a butterfly, Lord."

"Then why are you crawling around with the worms?"

"I don't know, Lord. It doesn't make much sense, does it?"

And then it is as if the Lord says, "I didn't make you into a new creature so that you could crawl around like a worm. I made you into a new creature so you could fly with the butterflies. Get up and fly."

God reasons with us in all areas of life. He doesn't condemn, because "there is now no condemnation for those who are in Christ Jesus" (Romans 8:1). He doesn't punish us for our sins because all the punishment was placed on Christ. There are natural repercussions to sin, but God keeps on renewing our minds with truth. When we agree with God concerning the truth and respond in faith, we will experience the abundant life He promised.

Mistakenly, we think that if we can quit sinning or if we can keep short accounts with God through 1 John 1:9, then we're okay. But this isn't God's way, according to His Word.

So if you as a child of God have been stealing, losing your temper, gossiping, or whatever sin you are trapped in, God's message to you is "Stop it!" You have a new Master and are no longer a slave to sin, but a friend of God. You are His child. Stealing, getting angry, gossiping, or whatever, is inconsistent with who you are. You are a butterfly—new, re-created by God to fly, not to crawl around with the worms anymore.

When we see ourselves in our prideful human nature, we recognize that our flesh resists grace and total forgiveness. It wants us to continue to deal with the sin issue, as if God hasn't already dealt with it totally. What we're saying is that Christ's death hasn't actually taken away all our sins, only those up to the day of our salvation. We reason that now that we are in Christ, it's up to us to walk the straight and narrow and to name our sins one by one.

What an affront to the cross!

God's provision for our sin isn't confession, and it isn't exhaling or inhaling. Rather, it's the renewal of our minds wherein He says, "If you've been stealing, turn to a better solution: Go to work, earn money, and share with others. If you've been using foul language, don't continue in that habit; rather, start a new habit of edifying one another."

What About Repentance?

Along with confession, a related question often asked is, "What is repentance?"

Most Christians think that repentance means they once did something bad and now they have turned from it and don't do it anymore. For example, "I used to smoke, but I repented and now I don't smoke anymore." But that's not entirely true. You could start again. The true meaning of repentance in the Bible is associated with salvation. When Jesus went into Galilee at the start of His ministry, He said, "The time has come! The kingdom of God is near. Repent and believe the good news!" (Mark 1:15).

Peter's salvation message in Acts 2:38,39 was, "Repent and be baptized, every one of you, in the name of Jesus Christ for the forgiveness of your sins. And you will receive the gift of the Holy Spirit. The promise is for you and your children and for all who are far off—for all whom the Lord our God will call."

Peter is saying that the same message of repentance is also for us. But once we've repented by turning from our unbelief to believing and receiving Christ, we can't re-repent. Repentance is changing our mind about the gospel. I was once an unbeliever; now I am a believer.

I liken it to a breakfast of bacon and eggs in the morning. The chicken made a contribution, but the pig made a total commitment. Repentance is pig stuff. It's a total change of mind from your lost condition to a firm conviction of relying on Christ as your Lord and Savior.

When you came to Christ, you turned from your old way of thinking. You repented of your unbelief and began a new life of faith in Jesus, allowing God to be on the throne of your life. You decreased; He increased. You emerged from the cocoon of slavery as a new creation. Now you are a butterfly. How can you ever go back to being an ugly, hairy worm? Why would you want to?

Christians get confused about confession and repentance because they're allowing their feelings to dictate their theology. In other words, they don't *feel* forgiven, so they want something to do that will change the way they feel. If they confess or have repented, as practiced in most churches today, they can feel comfortable that they've done what they were taught to do to get right with God. They want to feel good again. In other words, we prefer to walk by feeling rather than by faith.

I've checked my Bible over and over again to see what it says about feelings. What I have found is that the Bible is almost silent about feelings—especially when it comes to dealing with faith.

Feelings are always responders to thought. How much better do you think you'll feel by simply believing the truth? However, if you insist on feeling guilty and unforgiven, you'll slide into a feeling of depression that accompanies guilt. But if you set your faith on Jesus Christ and the total forgiveness of your sins, then your feelings will follow. You'll have the joy that comes from Him and the bonus of a clear conscience.

The truth is, if you are in Christ, you are a forgiven person. There is nothing more for you to do but to trust Him. You don't have to be preoccupied with sin and trying to get that black mark erased. That sin is history as far as God's concerned. He's forgotten all about it at the cross.

Faith is our response to God's truth. It is simply believing God. When I was confronted with the finality of the cross, I had to come to a point where I said, "Lord, I'm going to trust Your Word that when You say I'm forever forgiven, then I'm *forever forgiven*. And never again will I insult You by asking You to do for me what Your

Son has completed for me. Instead, I'm going to thank You forever for my eternal forgiveness in Christ." After I made this confession, my life has never been the same.

I've looked and looked at this forgiveness issue from every angle, and the only true response that faith would have us do is to say, "Thank You." I hope that having read these past several chapters you have come to the same understanding and conclusion, and that from this day forth you will live your life continually praising God for what He accomplished for you on the cross. I urge you to finalize what God has finished. You are a forgiven person!

Faith's Response to the Spirit's Leading

WHEN I FIRST CAME TO CHRIST, I was hungry to learn about the Lord. That is probably true of most people when they receive their new life in Christ. Soon, however, this new life begins to be choked out by the cares of this world, by the desires of the flesh, or by legalism, and the Christian life becomes a struggle. The joy we first experienced has turned to frustration and discouragement.

If there were just one word to use to describe the average Christian today, it would be *struggling*. We struggle to gain peace or to overcome sin. We struggle to live holy lives or to stay in good favor with God and man. Everything is a struggle. And in the midst of that struggle we want to know, "How can I stop doing the things I know I shouldn't?" But even deeper than that, what we really want to know is how we can enjoy the presence of Christ in our life. How can our faith respond daily to Christ in a way that will bring the joy we seek?

These were some of the questions a woman named Patricia wanted answered when she called our People to People radio broadcast. You could hear the emotion in her voice as she began, "Bob, I struggle with an eating disorder. The Lord gave me five years of freedom from it after I accepted Him. But for the last four years, my weight, health, nutrition, and exercise have become my focus. I'm obsessed with these things and I'm back in bondage again. As a child of the Lord, how can I be struggling like this, and how do I get out of this mess and become a mom to my kids and a pleasant wife to my husband again? I just don't know what to do."

Can you identify with Patricia? You may not be experiencing the same problem, but have you asked the question, "Why am I struggling like this?" Here was my answer to Patricia that evening.

"Patricia, I've seen this pattern in many people's lives, including my own. When we come to Christ, all we know is to depend on the love of God. That's what we respond to: 'Jesus loves me this I know, for the Bible tells me so.' We may not know much more than that, but the love of God is enough. Then, at some point we find ourselves struggling with some of the old desires again, whether it's alcohol, food, or whatever.

"What happens, Patricia, is that we start taking God's love for granted. We forget that the reason our lives changed in the first place is that we began depending totally on Him. But now the focus is back on us and what we're doing, instead of a preoccupation with Him and what He's doing."

I assured her that she wasn't unusual. We've all been there. As the conversation continued, Patricia kept asking whether or not she should exercise and how she should handle her nutrition. She kept wanting to know what to do. Finally, I said, "Patricia, you're missing the whole point. You're focusing on what you're doing instead of what has happened in your heart. You have become preoccupied with Patricia instead of who lives in you.

"And in so doing, you've allowed yourself to get back under your own laws of what you should look like. It's like Paul said in Romans 7:15: 'The things I want to do, I don't do, and the things I don't want to do, I do' " [my paraphrase].

She responded quickly, "Oh, yes! That's me! That's me!"

"Patricia, that's *all* of us," I said. "But don't stop reading there. Go on to read the solution: 'What a wretched man I am! Who will rescue me from this body of death? Thanks be to God—through Jesus Christ our Lord!' (Romans 7:24,25). You see, you don't come to Christ just to be forgiven. That's not the complete message of salvation. Salvation is receiving life—Christ's life—in you, the hope of glory. He gave His life for you, so that, raised from the dead, He could give His life *to* you, so that He could live His life *through* you. You and I can't live the Christian life; only He can."

God's answer to our struggle is Jesus. Just as we trusted Him for salvation by faith, we are to trust Him daily to live His life through us. As Patricia listened, she finally started to understand. Instead of trying to overcome her weakness through self-effort, she was going to start responding to the life of Christ living inside her and listening to Him and His direction in all things.

You see, His desire for us is to enjoy Him and the life He has provided. We can only do so as we respond by

faith. Paul tells us this in Galatians 2:20: "I have been cru-
cified with Christ and I no longer live, but Christ lives in
me. The life I live in the body, I live by faith in the Son of
God, who loved me and gave Himself for me."

Paul describes this life elsewhere in the Scriptures as
being led by the Spirit of God (Romans 8:14). We can
experience this by living moment by moment in total
dependence and trust on God.

That is the secret of the Christian life—total dependence on Christ. Proverbs 3:5,6 is one of my wife Amy's
favorite passages of Scripture because it so clearly com-
municates this truth: "Trust in the LORD with all your
heart, and lean not on your own understanding; in all
your ways acknowledge Him, and He will make your
paths straight."

Jesus taught this life of dependence to His disciples
by using the illustration of the vine and its branches. "I
am the vine; you are the branches. If a man remains in
Me and I in him, he will bear much fruit; apart from Me
you can do nothing" (John 15:5).

When we respond to the saving life of Christ by
faith—when we abide in Him as the vine, we find
freedom from our struggle to live the Christian life.

Freed from the Law

The first step in learning to abide in the vine is to
realize our freedom from the law of sin and death. In
Matthew 5:17 Jesus said, "Do not think that I have come
to abolish the Law or the Prophets; I have not come to
abolish them, but to fulfill them." In fulfilling them completely for us, He released us from the burden of trying

to fulfill what we could never do ourselves. By virtue of being "in Him," the law has been fulfilled on our behalf.

Christ didn't accomplish this for us because there was a flaw in the law. No, the law of God is perfect, but when it flows through us, it kills us. We are the flawed ones. But God in His mercy raised us from the dead and gave us His life. He has set in place a new law—one that supersedes the old: "Through Christ Jesus the law of the Spirit of life set me free from the law of sin and death" (Romans 8:2).

For a moment, think of the law of gravity as being analogous to the law of sin and death. We are bound by it because of its strength. And it's a law that has no end, as far as humanity is concerned.

There is also another law—one that overrides the law of gravity—and that's the law of aerodynamics. Birds overcome the law of gravity. So do well-designed aircraft, rockets, missiles, and even kites. Because it's much stronger, the law of aerodynamics overcomes the law of gravity. So, too, we see in Romans 8:2 that the "law of the Spirit of life" has triumphed over the Old Testament law of judgment.

How does this new law of liberty play out in real life and why is it so important? Because it affects the way we live as Christians. As children of God we are new creatures. We have a new identity, yet we are still housed in a body of flesh.

What it means is that now we have both spiritual and fleshly desires living next door to each other. It's easy for us to understand our fleshly desires. We grew up with them and learned to fulfill them instantly. And before we knew Christ, all that mattered was making sure those fleshly desires were satisfied. But now as born-again Christians, we have a new inhabitant with a new voice to listen to and a new set of desires. These new desires are not something we initiate; they come from God. For example, after I came to Christ I had a strong desire to share my discovery and joy with other people. I didn't conjure up that desire, and it certainly wasn't there before I knew Jesus. God placed that desire in my heart. All I had to do was respond.

Many Christians come to me for counsel concerning their personal problems. What I usually find is that they already know the answer. Their struggle is in letting go of fulfilling the desires of the flesh and instead tuning in and responding to what God has already put in their hearts.

To illustrate, let's say someone you work with offends you in some way. The natural fleshly response is to get even. For a lost person, that's the most logical option. But as a child of God, there is a different voice—a desire of the Spirit that leads to a better way. This new desire reasons with us to go to the person who wronged us and straighten out the situation. At this point, we have a choice. Do we want to give in to the flesh or listen to the Spirit of God? Are we willing to walk by faith and obey the desires of the Spirit? The encouragement of the Scriptures is this: "Since we live by the Spirit, let us keep in step with the Spirit" (Galatians 5:25).

We often fail to respond because we think we know what is best for us. Our pride gets in the way. But as we grow in our understanding of God's love for us, we discover that God's ways are always best. And so our dependency on Christ deepens.

As our dependence strengthens, we find a greater willingness to obey Him. Most Christians want to obey God, but the only way that pleases Him is when we trust

Him. Otherwise, we find ourselves trying to obey God out of a hidden fear of punishment or because we've gone back to a form of legalism. True obedience is a natural by-product of a pulsating dependence on Christ.

Obedience apart from dependency is legalism. First John 4:19 says it in these words: "We love because He first loved us." When we are convinced of God's love for us, we respond rightly. A person can't have a love for God in his or her heart unless he or she knows and experiences God's love. On the radio, in church, in Christian meetings, we constantly are hammered to be "obedient" to God and threatened with the consequences if we aren't. But obedience is a natural result of love, not a legalistic obligation.

So the order of the Christian life is this: God's love for us, which results in our love for God, which results in our dependence on God, which results in our obedience to God. When we approach the Christian life in this order, we are free to enjoy life without fear.

That Christian believers struggle to please God through obedience to the law isn't new at all. Remember those "foolish Galatians" of the first century?

Down through history and to this present day, there are groups of believers who are two-timing—they have one foot in Christ and the other in the law. But there are also many fine, single-minded men and women of God who *do* understand the saving life of Christ. One that I admire greatly is Major Ian Thomas, founder of the Torchbearers Ministry. As I mentioned in chapter 3, he wrote a best-selling book years ago entitled *The Saving Life of Christ*. That wonderful book has become a classic, and deservedly so. I recommend it highly.

Not Me, I Would Never Commit Murder

Recently, I had a discussion with a young lady about a murder story she had read in a newspaper.

"I don't understand how someone could do such a thing," she said. "I could never kill anyone. Not me."

"That's interesting," I answered. "Then you only need 90 percent of Jesus, and if it were impossible for you to steal, then you would only need 80 percent of Jesus. And maybe one day you could become so good, you wouldn't need Jesus at all." She looked at me—she got my point.

To really grasp the extent of God's grace and to respond to the life of Christ, we must understand the extent of our fallen nature, our sinfulness, and our depravity. The truth is, *there is not a sin under the sun that you or I couldn't commit, given the right set of circumstances.* That is the truth about ourselves that God wants us to see and understand. We should never say, "I don't understand how someone could do that." That is a self-righteous attitude rooted in pride. Our real attitude should be, "But for the grace of God, there go I."

What will bring us to this attitude? Coming to grips with the root of all sin. We always deal with the fruit, but God deals with the root. For example, He said that to lust after a woman was the same as actually committing the act. Now, that statement alone ought to lay bare our hearts before God.

Jesus, who is God, was driving home the truth that all sin originates in our heart. To remedy sin, we must have a heart transplant. It's for certain that if there's one thing the law could never do, it's to change a person's heart. Only God could do that for us. The prophet Ezekiel wrote, "I will give you a new heart and put a new spirit

in you; I will remove from you your h
give you a heart of flesh" (Ezekiel 36:2(
God, we have a new heart: *His* heart.

No, the law couldn't give us a new h
intended it to. He gave the law to show us
Friend, we are totally blind to our wretche   ௨ιαι we
look squarely into the mirror of the law. Think of Paul's
life before Jesus met with him on the road to Damascus.
He was a Pharisee of Pharisees, and concerning legalistic
righteousness, he said he was faultless. This mind-set
blinded him to his spiritual condition, so much so that he
thought by persecuting Christians he was carrying out
the will of God. I guess he overlooked commandment
number six—the one that says, "Do not murder."

But finally, the law did its work in Paul's life and he
saw the true condition of his heart. In Romans 7:7-13, he
shares what the law revealed in him:

> What shall we say, then? Is the law sin? Certainly
> not! Indeed I would not have known what sin
> was except through the law. For I would not
> have known what coveting really was if the law
> had not said, "Do not covet." But sin, seizing the
> opportunity afforded by the commandment,
> produced in me every kind of covetous desire.
> For apart from law, sin is dead. Once I was alive
> apart from law; but when the commandment
> came, sin sprang to life and I died. I found that
> the very commandment that was intended to
> bring life actually brought death. *For sin, seizing
> the opportunity afforded by the commandment,
> deceived me, and through the commandment put me
> to death.* So then, the law is holy, and the com-
> mandment is holy, righteous and good. Did that

which is good, then, become death to me? By no means! *But in order that sin might be recognized as sin, it produced death in me through what was good, so that through the commandment sin might become utterly sinful* (emphasis added).

Many of the early Hebrew Christians didn't understand the purpose of the law, so they found it difficult to let go of what they had been strictly trained in all their lives. Their response to Christ was to come to Him by faith, but then they continued to go back to the habit of living by the law. Paul said,

> But the Scripture declares that the whole world is a prisoner of sin, so that what was promised, being given through faith in Jesus Christ, might be given to those who believe. Before this faith came, we were held prisoners by the law, locked up until faith should be revealed. So the law was put in charge to lead us to Christ that we might be justified by faith. Now that faith has come, we are no longer under the supervision of the law (Galatians 3:22-25).

How much clearer can it get? If you are in Christ, you are no longer under the supervision of the law.

Under the law, you are a prisoner of sin and totally controlled by the desires of the flesh. Christ freed us from this old way of life. Yet these early Hebrew Christians went back to the law, and when they did, they returned to bondage and to the control and power of sin.

Sin deceives. And these Hebrew Christians were deceived into thinking they could produce godly works through obedience to the law. The flesh will *never* produce anything that pleases God. The flesh can produce religious works, yes, but never anything godly. And there is a huge difference between the two. Paul warned against this and urged the Galatians to "stand firm...and do not let yourselves be burdened again by a yoke of slavery" (Galatians 5:1).

These words are for us as well. We must let go of our religiosity, traditions, and observances that hinder us from responding to God's leading. He wants to strip away all our religion so that our dependence is stayed on Jesus. Christ is our life now, and He is far greater than all our traditions. "Therefore, if anyone is in Christ, he is a new creation; the old has gone, the new has come!" (2 Corinthians 5:17).

Concerning our freedom in Christ, Martin Luther in his *Treatise on Christian Liberty* wrote these compelling words:

> It is impossible for a man to be a Christian without having Christ. And if he has Christ, he has at the same time all that is in Christ. What gives peace to the conscience is that by faith our sins are no more ours, but Christ's, upon whom God hath laid them all. And that on the other hand all of Christ's righteousness is ours to whom God hath given it.
>
> Faith unites the soul with Christ, as a spouse with her husband. Everything which Christ has becomes the property of the believing soul. Everything which the soul has becomes the property of Christ. Christ possesses all blessings and eternal life and they are therefore the property of the soul. The soul has all its iniquities and

sins and they therefore become the property of Christ.

It is then a blessed exchange that happens. So that Christ who is both God and man, Christ who has never sinned, Christ whose holiness is perfect, Christ the almighty and eternal, taking to Himself by the nuptial ring of faith all the sins of the believer, those sins are lost and abolished in Him, for no sins dwell before the infinite righteousness of God. So the believer's soul is delivered from sin and clothed with eternal righteousness as the bridegroom of Christ.

If we could only grasp and understand the newness of life we have in Christ and the freedom that is ours by being led by His Spirit. But we hold tightly to the familiar, to that which is comfortable. This is true of the organized church as well. Most of the activities in our denominational churches are nothing more than traditions passed down from generation to generation. Rather than trusting the Lord to lead the members of a church in a fresh, new way, we repeat and continue doing things the same old way because "that's the way we have always done it." Through these traditions, we've organized the Holy Spirit right out of our Christian experience.

Let's refocus. All that matters in the Christian life is Jesus. He is our only hope. He is a blessed relief from the performance mode of legalism that tries to make the flesh feel good by what it does.

But when we serve a God whom we think is demanding of us, we soon realize we can't keep up with the demands. We try, but somehow our flesh can't behave perfectly, and so we hide our inner life and imperfections from each other.

As we go on in life, more than likely we get frustrated with people forcing us to be what we know deep down we are not. It's like living with someone who constantly notices what we do wrong and expects perfection in everything. Ultimately, we want to run away from such a taskmaster and find a place where we can be ourselves. If you are caught in such a trap, let me encourage you to run into the arms of Christ.

He *knows* you. He knows your weaknesses and the nature of your flesh. You don't have to pretend to be someone you're not. He knows better. Once we realize the truth that "apart from [Him we] can do nothing" (John 15:5), we are ready to respond to His life in us.

Paul's Test of a Christian

When an instructor is trying to teach an important lesson, repetition becomes critical for retention. Educators tell us we must hear something ten times before we really get the idea and it becomes part of us. This is true of even the most basic lessons.

A coach with a losing team won't launch new plays until he gets his players back to the basics of the game, practicing the plays and skills they should already know. In basketball the basic drills include dribbling, passing the ball, and shooting baskets. In baseball, it's throwing the ball where you want it to go, catching the ball, and having batting practice. Each sport has its own set of basics that are crucial to winning. The team that wins is always the one that has learned to execute the basics better than the other team.

The apostle Paul understood this principle and used it to illustrate spiritual truth. As he wrote to the Philippians, he included in chapter 3 these interesting words:

"It is no trouble for me to write the same things to you again, and it is a safeguard for you" (Philippians 3:1). We don't know, of course, when Paul first instructed the Philippians in the Christian life, but here he is again, going through the basics once more as a "safeguard." Why? Because we are so prone to forget.

As we continue to grow in grace, the foundational truths are necessities we need to return to. Many times we want to go on to deeper things, but the foundation is usually the deepest and strongest part of any solid structure. But if we get preoccupied with the doors and windows and the gingerbread trim, we're apt to forget the foundation.

Paul warns the Philippians to watch out for "those dogs...those mutilators of the flesh." These were the legalists among them who were insisting that new believers be circumcised according to the Jewish law. But Paul says, "It is we who are the circumcision, we who worship by the Spirit of God, who glory in Christ Jesus, and who put no confidence in the flesh" (Philippians 3:3). The circumcision Paul refers to is one of the heart—a "circumcision done by Christ" (Colossians 2:11). What is done in the flesh by man is of no value to God.

The reason we must be well-grounded in the basics is because false prophets always want to destroy the basic tenets of the faith, to destroy the foundation. Cults will try to do away with the deity of Christ, the plan of salvation, the resurrection, the assurance of eternal life, or some other basic doctrine of the faith. Liberal theology leans on human understanding to interpret biblical truth. Those who follow liberal theology have no idea what it is to be led and taught by the Holy Spirit of God, and so they interpret the virgin birth, the resurrection, or the sinfulness of mankind totally from a human perspective. If they can get people off the firm foundation, then all that follows will crumble. If a building's foundation is flawed, the whole building becomes unstable.

In his safeguarding message, Paul points out three signs of a true believer. While some people might say it's someone who has stopped sinning, or who attends church regularly, or who does good by being charitable, or who behaves with integrity, Paul has a different definition of a born-again believer. He says first that believers are, "we who worship by the Spirit of God" (Philippians 3:3).

The Worship Response

What does it mean to worship by the Spirit of God? Is it swinging and swaying to some melodic chorus repeated over and over? If you have 100,000 Christians in an arena singing their hearts out, does that constitute worship? Does raising your hands show you are worshiping? Then what about a person who is disabled, paralyzed, or has no tongue or arms? Is that person disqualified from worshiping God?

Some Christians confuse worship with emotional feelings; they like "spiritual goose bumps." A lady called our radio broadcast and asked me how she could make sure to get those "spiritual goose bumps" every time she attends church. These people believe that some feeling or ecstatic experience is the goal in Christian worship. But Jesus never mentioned emotions when He talked with the woman at the well: "True worshipers will worship the Father in spirit and truth, for they are the kind of worshipers the Father seeks" (John 4:23).

Worship that depends on emotional "highs" or feelings leads a person away from walking by faith. Their dependence shifts. But truth is objective. When we believe in Him whom God has sent, when we respond to and obey the truth, we're expressing the kind of worship God desires. Paul, in writing to the Roman Christians, encouraged true worship this way: "In view of God's mercy...offer your bodies as living sacrifices, holy and pleasing to God—this is your spiritual act of worship" (Romans 12:1). So for Paul, true worship was demonstrated by the presenting of the believer's body as a living sacrifice to God. In other words, the believer surrenders to God to be used by Him in any way He pleases. It's interesting that there's not a single reference in that verse—or anywhere else in the Scriptures—to emotion or ecstatic feelings as a sign of worship.

I realize that it's human nature to want to hold on to that which is familiar, to what we have always done. If we're used to certain feelings equating to worship, it's hard to think otherwise. This is true of any religious tradition to which we've become accustomed. I know a man who said with pride and enthusiasm, "I was born Baptist, I'll die Baptist, and if you stab me, I'll bleed Baptist."

You can insert any denominational label into that statement and find many people who are dyed-in-the-wool adherents to their tradition. It seems like God Himself can't pry them loose from their habits. Their theme is, "If you feel good in church, then everything's okay between you and God. But if you wake up depressed the next day, then somehow the connection to God is lost."

Emotion-based worship caters to and feeds the religious flesh. And like all appetites of the flesh, it is never satisfied. It always seeks more, some new experience. But God didn't tell us to renew our emotions. He said to be "transformed by the renewing of your mind" (Romans 12:2). God aims His truth at the mind, not the emotions; because the mind is the activator of our emotions. Proverbs 23:7 (NASB) puts it this way: "As [a man] thinks within himself, so he is." A renewed mind produces renewed emotions. But never let your feelings lead the way. Don't let the cart lead instead of the horse.

Those who rely on ritual as worship may also be uncomfortable realizing that true worship has nothing to do with repetitive prayers or lighting candles or bodily exercises. Again, it's easy to understand that if you have been brought up doing things a certain way in the church, it's hard to let go and start anew.

But when we consider Paul's admonition to present our bodies as living sacrifices to God, we see that true worship has more to do with daily living than with an hour on Sunday morning. Some Christians who present their bodies to God might find themselves on the mission field or in full-time ministry, but others will find God using their bodies to fulfill His plan as businessmen, mothers, teachers, or whatever plan He has for each life.

Glory in Christ Jesus

The second mark of a Christian, Paul mentions, is that he or she "glories in Christ Jesus." A true Christian will want to make Christ known to other people. When He is lifted up, He'll draw all men unto Himself.

A sincere witness cares about other people and tries to understand their needs. If you take enough time to talk to someone, you'll discover that person's need and find a way to introduce him to Christ. You'll be able to share in love the hope that is within you in a way that relates to that individual's problem.

A true witness, by the way, "glories in Christ Jesus," not in the Holy Spirit. If you focus more on talking about the Holy Spirit than Jesus, you are off base scripturally. God sent the Holy Spirit to testify about Jesus and to give boldness to the disciples to preach the gospel. The Holy Spirit never calls attention to Himself, but to Jesus. That should be our attitude also.

The third mark of a believer is that he "puts no confidence in the flesh." When we finally understand that in our flesh we can do nothing that will impress God, then we can say, "God, it's all You and none of me." Paul says he would have had reason to put confidence in the flesh, but instead he counts his entire former life of adherence to the law as "loss compared to the surpassing greatness of knowing Christ Jesus" (Philippians 3:8).

If Paul wanted to brag, his resumé of works would have impressed any legalist. But he chose to liken his accomplishments to that of rubbish compared to knowing Christ.

What About Prayer?

What about prayer, you ask? Doesn't God respond to our prayers by giving us what we ask for? Don't we trigger God's action through our prayers? Isn't that the whole purpose of prayer—getting God to do something for us or to stop something bad from happening?

No. Prayer, rightly understood, is a *response* to God, to the leading of His Spirit, not an attempt to initiate God's action. The purest prayers we pray are prayers God has put first on our heart. He initiates prayer by giving us His desires and a heart to pray as we should. We read in 1 John 5:14,15: "This is the confidence we have in approaching God: that if we ask anything according to His will, He hears us. And if we know that He hears us—whatever we ask—we know that we have what we asked of Him."

Thus, when we pray, we're simply asking God to do what He has already willed or initiated. He has given us the desire of His heart. Our prayers are expressions of what God wants to do. He initiates; we respond.

In James we're told that "the prayer of a righteous man is powerful and effective. Elijah was a man just like us. He prayed earnestly that it would not rain, and it did not rain on the land for three and a half years. Again he prayed, and the heavens gave rain, and the earth produced its crops" (James 5:16-18).

What a powerful prayer! Most of us read this and say, "I wish I could pray as effectively as Elijah." But did Elijah initiate this prayer? Did it originate in his heart? Let's take a closer look.

His prayers were powerful and effective because they came straight from the Word of God. In Deuteronomy 11:16,17, God said to the people of Israel, "Be careful, or you will be enticed to turn away and worship other gods and bow down to them. Then the LORD's anger will burn against you, and he *will shut the heavens so that it will not rain and the ground will yield no produce,* and you will soon perish from the good land the LORD is giving you" (emphasis added).

When Elijah was on the scene, Israel had turned away from the Lord and was worshiping Baal. So according to God's Word, Elijah prayed that it would not rain. For three years it did not rain.

Elijah prayed again for the rain to start because the Lord had said He would send rain: "After a long time, in the third year, the word of the LORD came to Elijah: 'Go and present yourself to Ahab, and I will send rain on the land'" (1 Kings 18:1). Elijah's prayers were powerful *because God through His Word initiated them.* Our prayers can be just as powerful and effective if we step aside and let God be the initiator in our heart through His Word.

Our True Identity

The new covenant has secured for all those "in Christ" a new identity—that of a forgiven, new creation (2 Corinthians 5:17), perfect in God's sight. The Christian who daily rests in his or her new identity is content and happy like the butterfly that has emerged from a dark cocoon. Even though we know this, it is very easy to slip back into the old way of thinking.

Frequently we hear the comment, "But we still have to be obedient to the law." And most people who say this are referring to the Ten Commandments. They will agree we are not under the "ceremonial law," but they will argue until they are blue in the face that we still have to keep the Big Ten. Friend, again we have to look at what the Bible says concerning the law:

> He has made us competent as ministers of a new covenant—not of the letter but of the Spirit; for the letter kills, but the Spirit gives life. Now if

the ministry that brought death, which was
engraved in letters on stone, came with glory, so
that the Israelites could not look steadily at the
face of Moses because of its glory, fading though
it was, will not the ministry of the Spirit be even
more glorious? (2 Corinthians 3:6-8).

Notice Paul is talking about the Ten Commandments.
The law that kills is that which was engraved in letters
on stone. We are no longer under that law. We have been
set free from it by the Spirit of life.

But to those who persist, what will their obedience to
the law accomplish? It will either make them prideful
and pleased with self, or self-condemnation will heap
guilt in their heart because of the realization of falling
short of God's best. God never meant for us to live this
way. He gave us a new life, and we are to be led exclusively by His Spirit.

No, friend, there is no righteousness available through
obedience to the law or through anything we do. The
only righteousness God looks for is in Christ. And if we
have Him, we have the righteousness that comes from
God and is by faith. So what is there for us to do? Only
to stop trying and to start trusting!

God fulfilled our need for righteousness by grace
through faith in Jesus Christ. Once we are embracing
Christ and His total provision for us, it's hard to understand how anyone could turn away from such a magnificent gift from God.

E. Stanley Jones was one of the great Christian leaders
of the past century. For decades, Jones served the Lord
Jesus Christ as a missionary to India.

As he began one of his new books, he tells what he wanted to find:

> ...some concept that would reduce the whole of life to the utmost simplicity. If you have that, you're "in"; if you don't have it, you're "out." By "in" I mean "in life," and by "out," "out of life." I felt I had found that concept in the phrase "in Christ." If you are "in Christ," you're "in life"; if you are "out of Christ," you're "out of life." If that proposition is true, then it cuts down through all veneer, all seeming, all make-believe, all marginalisms, all half-wayisms—through everything—and brings us to the ultimate essence of things: If you are "in Christ," you are in life; if you are "out of Christ," you're out of life, here and now, and hereafter.

Jones went on to point out how a person might be interested in religion or even the church, but yet not be "in Christ." Listen to Jones again:

> The phrase "in Christ" is the ultimate phrase in the Christian faith, for it locates us in a Person— the Divine Person—and it locates us in Him here and now. It brings us to the ultimate relationship—"in." Obviously this "in" brings us nearer than "near Christ," "following Christ," "believing in Christ," or even "committed to Christ." You cannot go further or deeper than "in."

Throughout the epistles of the New Testament, Paul (and the other New Testament writers) frequently used the phrase "in Christ" as a way of describing the believers who were receiving the letter as a reminder of what their inheritance is and what they now possess in Christ.

Many Christians who choose to hang on to the millstone of the law will never experience the peace of God or the contentment that Christ offers. Forever they will be wondering if they have been "good enough" for God to accept them. Bogged down in the pit of self-effort, they will miss the joy of responding to the life of Christ.

If you are in Christ, then you have Christ living in your heart. He is there to renew your mind with truth and to produce in and through you the fruit of His Spirit. Peter says this in 2 Peter 1:3,4:

> His divine power has given us everything we need for life and godliness through our knowledge of him who called us by his own glory and goodness. Through these he has given us his very great and precious promises, so that through them you may participate in the divine nature and escape the corruption in the world caused by evil desires.

He has come to live in you so that you can participate in the divine nature. What a privilege! And it's available to anyone who responds to Christ's saving life by faith.

One Faith for All Men

SEVERAL YEARS AGO I HAD the privilege of traveling to Greece. I toured Athens and stood on Mars Hill, where Paul addressed the Greek philosophers in Acts 17. "Men of Athens," he said, "I see that in every way you are very religious. For as I walked around and looked carefully at your objects of worship, I even found an altar with this inscription: TO AN UNKNOWN GOD. Now what you worship as something unknown I am going to proclaim to you" (Acts 17:22,23).

I then traveled to Corinth and saw the site where the Corinthians built a temple to honor Aphrodite, the goddess of love. Right next to where this temple stood, archaeologists have uncovered a Star of David laid out in mosaic. Until Paul brought the gospel message, a small group of Jews was the only voice of the one true God in a world of paganism.

This trip was very significant in my spiritual growth, as was my first trip to Israel. I never realized how depraved the Gentile culture was in that day. Everything they did, they did to excess. The word *moderation* was not in their vocabulary. They worshiped temple prostitutes and idols of every kind. Homosexuality was rampant. There were no restraints on the flesh at all. We think our society is bad in America. We have yet a long way to go to match the debauchery and evil that reigned in the Gentile culture of Paul's day.

Seeing the heathen roots of my Gentile heritage was quite an eye-opener, but more importantly, it deepened my understanding of the Word of God. As I read through the New Testament, I started seeing how often the writers referred to Jew and Gentile. The book of Acts is the story of God first reaching out to the Jews, and then through Paul, reaching out to the Gentiles. One of the main themes of the books of Romans and Ephesians is God's plan to save both Jew and Gentile by the same means. I also noticed that when the Bible talks about Jew and Gentile, it also talks about predestination and election. All of a sudden I saw that predestination isn't about who is chosen for salvation and who is not. It is about God's plan to make one new body of believers from both Jew and Gentile.

Until this time, predestination was a subject I wanted to avoid altogether. You have the Calvinists on one side saying salvation is only for the elect few who have been predestined by God to receive it. On the other hand, you have the Arminians saying it's available to all who will exercise their free will and believe of their own accord. Both groups are so adamant about their position that it seems impossible to carry on a civil discussion.

People call me on the radio broadcast and proudly announce, "I'm a Calvinist," or "I'm an Arminian," and then they proceed to ask their question. I always wonder why people label themselves in this way. When you think about it, if Calvin had anything to say, he didn't come up with the information originally. It came from the apostle Paul, and I don't think Calvin called himself a Paulinist.

If he had, Paul would have chastised him just like he did the Corinthians. In Corinth, there were people proudly saying, "'I follow Paul'; another, 'I follow Apollos'; another, 'I follow Cephas'; still another, 'I follow Christ'" (1 Corinthians 1:12). Paul confronted this head-on by asking,

> Is Christ divided? Was Paul crucified for you? Were you baptized into the name of Paul?... What, after all, is Apollos? And what is Paul? Only servants, through whom you came to believe—as the Lord has assigned to each his task. I planted the seed, Apollos watered it, but God made it grow. So neither he who plants nor he who waters is anything, but only God, who makes things grow (1 Corinthians 1:13; 3:5-7).

Wouldn't Calvin and Arminius fall in this same category? Aren't they just servants?

When we label ourselves according to what certain people espouse and believe, we do nothing but divide the body of Christ. With the lines drawn between Calvinists and Arminians, the subject of predestination has become highly divisive. Yet, when you see what the Bible really says about this subject, it becomes the most unifying doctrine in all the Scriptures. So let's take a closer look at predestination and election and see how faith responds to this unifying message.

The Backdrop

For all practical purposes, the church began on the Day of Pentecost. Jews traveled from every nation to

Jerusalem to celebrate this feast. Peter and the other 11 disciples, filled with the Holy Spirit, miraculously communicated the gospel in the native languages of those attending the feast. The people were utterly amazed to hear these Galileans proclaim the wonders of God in their own language.

Then Peter stood and addressed the crowd. He fervently preached on the death, burial, and resurrection of Jesus. At the end, he urged his listeners to repent and receive the Holy Spirit. That day, 3,000 Jews believed the gospel and were added to the church. The *ekklesia*, or "called-out ones," or what we know as the church was formed, and it was made up exclusively of Jewish converts. This is how it remained until Cornelius, a Gentile and a Roman centurion, summoned Peter to Caesarea to communicate the gospel to him.

We pick up the story in Acts 10. Peter was in the town of Joppa staying with a tanner named Simon. About noon one day, Peter went up on the roof to pray. He fell into a trance and

> ...saw heaven opened and something like a large sheet being let down to earth by its four corners. It contained all kinds of four-footed animals, as well as reptiles of the earth and birds of the air. Then a voice told him, "Get up, Peter. Kill and eat." "Surely not, Lord!" Peter replied. "I have never eaten anything impure or unclean." The voice spoke to him a second time, "Do not call anything impure that God has made clean" (Acts 10:11-15).

Peter didn't understand what the vision meant, but as he pondered it, three men sent by Cornelius stopped at the gate of Simon's house and asked for him. After explaining why they had come, they escorted Peter to Caesarea. As Peter entered Cornelius's house, he said to them, "You are well aware that it is against our law for a Jew to associate with a Gentile or visit him. But God has shown me that I should not call any man impure or unclean. So when I was sent for, I came without raising any objection. May I ask why you sent for me?" (Acts 10:28,29). It was against Jewish law for Peter to even associate with Cornelius, much less visit him. In the Jewish way of thinking, the Gentile was impure and unclean.

Try to imagine what it was like for Peter and the first-century Jew to think that their God, Jehovah, the great "I AM," was now including and offering salvation to those pagan Gentiles, to heathens! Even more appalling was the thought and teaching that the God of the Jews was now dwelling in the hearts of those awful, unclean Gentiles. And even worse—if it could get any worse in the eyes of a first-century Jew—was the teaching that the Gentiles, through the Spirit of God, now had access to the Holy of Holies (Hebrews 10:19). This idea, for the Jew, was abhorrent.

But Peter was listening to God teach him truth. He realized "that God does not show favoritism." So he began proclaiming the good news of Jesus Christ. When he spoke these words: "All the prophets testify about Him that everyone who believes in Him receives forgiveness of sins through His name" (Acts 10:43), the Holy Spirit came on Cornelius and all who heard the message. A Gentile had received the Holy Spirit just as the Jews had. The Jewish believers who were with Peter were stunned. As Luke writes, they "were astonished that the gift of the Holy Spirit had been poured out even on the Gentiles" (Acts 10:45). They never dreamed in a million years that Gentiles would be included in the gospel and be offered the Holy Spirit.

Peter traveled back to Jerusalem to tell the believers there what had happened. At first they criticized him for going into Cornelius's home. They couldn't believe he broke the Jewish law. But Peter explained the whole story. He concluded with this: "So if God gave them the same gift as he gave us, who believed in the Lord Jesus Christ, who was I to think that I could oppose God?" (Acts 11:17). After the Jerusalem believers heard Peter's conclusion, they responded by saying, "So then, God has granted even the Gentiles repentance unto life" (Acts 11:18).

Until that time, the believers in Jerusalem and those who had been scattered because of persecution had shared the message of Jesus Christ only with Jews. They thought it was exclusively a Jewish message. But once they realized the Gentiles could now also be saved by believing in the Jewish Messiah, they began to proclaim the good news to Jew and Gentile alike. They responded by faith to the truth of God's plan that had been *predestined* from the beginning. The message was this: "Whosoever will may come." And now the church was made up of Jews *and* Gentiles who had come to Christ the same way—by faith.

The Mystery Revealed

If you ask the average person on the street today what the opposite of a Jew is, most everyone would answer, "a Christian." But the truth is that the opposite of a Jew is a *Gentile*, not a Christian. These two categories, Jew and Gentile, comprise the lost world, from God's point of view.

But out of these two groups of people, God's plan was to create a third group called the church or, in Greek, *ekklesia*.

> His purpose was to create in himself one new man out of the two, thus making peace, and in this one body to reconcile both of them to God through the cross, by which he put to death their hostility. He came and preached peace to you who were far away [Gentile] and peace to those who were near [Jew]. For through him we both have access to the Father by one Spirit (Ephesians 2:15-18).

This "one new [spiritual] man" is to be made up of both Jew and Gentile who come to Christ by faith. So from God's vantage point, there are three groups of people: Jews, Gentiles, and born-again believers—made up of both Jews and Gentiles—whom we call Christians. This new group, called the church, was a mystery which was held in the heart of God until it was revealed by the Holy Spirit to Peter, Paul, and the rest of the apostles.

The mystery, as Paul explained, is this: "Through the gospel the Gentiles are heirs together with Israel, members together of one body, and sharers together in the promise in Christ Jesus" (Ephesians 3:6). In God's plan, from the beginning, the Gentiles were *predestined* to receive the same salvation as the Jew. The Gentile world was predestined to come to Christ in the identical way as the Jew, and the Jew would be saved the same way as the Gentile. As we have seen, that was a radical thought to the mostly Jewish New Testament believers. Nevertheless, this was God's plan. Look how He includes both Jew and Gentile in the following passage:

> In Him we were also chosen, having been pre-destined according to the plan of Him who works out everything in conformity with the purpose of His will, in order that we [Jews], who were the first to hope in Christ, might be for the praise of His glory. And you [Gentiles] also were included in Christ when you heard the word of truth, the gospel of your salvation. Having believed, you were marked in Him with a seal, the promised Holy Spirit, who is a deposit guaranteeing our inheritance until the redemption of those who are God's possession—to the praise of His glory (Ephesians 1:11-14).

The doctrine of predestination (or election, as it's also called) is not about "you" and "me." It's about God's plan to offer salvation to all humanity, both to the Jew and the Gentile. The more I read through the book of Ephesians, the clearer this wonderful message became. I wondered, "How have we missed this? Why have we misapplied the doctrine of predestination and allowed it to become such a tool of division in the body of Christ?"

Part of the problem is that we pick and choose verses that support our particular slant on the issue and never look at the big picture. Each side of the argument has its particular set of verses to camp on. But it's interesting that neither side discusses the context of these verses.

When we look at the business of real estate, we see three rules for success. They are location, location, and location. The same is true for Bible study. The three rules are context, context, and context. I encourage people to read large portions of Scripture at a time to fully see the context. Rather than reading a few verses, read through an entire book. If you have a question about a specific verse, read through the entire book again, and you will probably find your answer in light of the big picture.

Reading through the books of Ephesians and Romans, you see that the context of the verses that speak to the doctrines of predestination and election is all about God's plan to save both Jew and Gentile. And as I have said numerous times on our radio broadcast, when understood in context, it becomes as clear as the nose on your face. When you see God's plan, you can't help but marvel at the depth of God's wisdom and rejoice in what He has done. Only God could bring about such powerful results in making the two into one, which we read in Ephesians 2:11-13,19-21 and Colossians 3:11:

> Therefore, remember that formerly you who are Gentiles by birth and called "uncircumcised" by those who call themselves "the circumcision" (that done in the body by the hands of men)— remember that at that time you were separate from Christ, excluded from citizenship in Israel and foreigners to the covenants of the promise, without hope and without God in the world. But now in Christ Jesus you who once were far away have been brought near through the blood of Christ....Consequently, you are no longer foreigners and aliens, but fellow citizens with God's

people and members of God's household, built
on the foundation of the apostles and prophets,
with Christ Jesus Himself as the chief corner-
stone. In Him the whole building is joined
together and rises to become a holy temple in the
Lord....Here there is no Greek or Jew, circumcised or uncircumcised, barbarian, Scythian,
slave or free, but Christ is all, and is in all.

God foreknew what would take place with the Jew
and Gentile. Galatians 3:8,9 says, "The Scripture foresaw that God would justify the Gentiles by faith, and
announced the gospel in advance to Abraham: 'All
nations will be blessed through you.' So those who
have faith are blessed along with Abraham, the man
of faith." For those who would come to Him by faith,
He predestined "to be conformed to the likeness of his
Son" (Romans 8:29).

What a marvelous plan! Before we go on, let me high-
light some of the main points we have discussed thus
far.

- There are only three categories of people
  from God's perspective: Jews, Gentiles, and the
  ekklesia—the called-out ones from both Jews and
  Gentiles.

- The *ekklesia* is made up of both Jews and Gentiles
  who by faith have been born again by the Spirit of
  God.

- All Jews and Gentiles who have come to Him by
  faith have been predestined to be conformed into
  the image of Christ Jesus.

- The purpose of God's predestination, election, and choosing is that both Jew and Gentile would be made into one new spiritual body through faith in Jesus Christ.

- He predestined, elected, and chose that whosoever comes to Him by faith will by no means be cast aside (John 6:37).

Misunderstanding God's Mystery

The Jews were not thrilled with this plan. They wanted the gospel to be exclusively theirs. But Paul knew better. Wherever he traveled, he reasoned with both Jew and Gentile concerning the gospel. The more the Gentiles responded, the more resentful the Jews became. This frustrated Paul, because his greatest desire was for his fellow countrymen to be saved.

Even though Paul told the Jews on several occasions that he was going exclusively to the Gentiles because they would listen, wherever he traveled he went first to his brothers in the synagogue in hopes that some would come to know Christ. He expressed his deep concern for his people in Romans 9:1-4: "I speak the truth in Christ—I am not lying, my conscience confirms it in the Holy Spirit—I have great sorrow and unceasing anguish in my heart. For I could wish that I myself were cursed and cut off from Christ for the sake of my brothers, those of my own race, the people of Israel."

It would have been easy for Paul to succumb to the pressure the Jews placed on him, but he never compromised the message. In the book of Romans, he presents the most complete and logical treatise on God's plan of salvation for both Jew and Gentile.

Let's look at some key passages throughout the book to see how God's plan unfolds. First, we see that the gospel is for everyone who believes. It's not a Jewish gospel, nor is it a Gentile gospel. "I am not ashamed of the gospel, because it is the power of God for the salvation of everyone who believes: first for the Jew, then for the Gentile" (Romans 1:16).

However, for someone to respond to Christ by faith, he must first see his need for salvation. This is where the Jews misunderstood God's plan. They knew the Gentile sinners needed a Savior, but *they* were already God's chosen people. They were in, so they thought, by virtue of their heritage. But Paul in his logical way proved that the Jew was under the condemnation of sin, just as the Gentile was.

> A man is not a Jew if he is only one outwardly, nor is circumcision merely outward and physical. No, a man is a Jew if he is one inwardly; and circumcision is circumcision of the heart, by the Spirit, not by the written code. Such a man's praise is not from men, but from God (Romans 2:28,29).

> What shall we conclude then? Are we any better? Not at all! We have already made the charge that Jews and Gentiles alike are all under sin. As it is written, "There is no one righteous, not even one" (Romans 3:9,10).

Then Paul boldly proclaimed the solution by showing how all men could be justified freely by God's grace through faith in Jesus Christ:

This righteousness from God comes through faith in Jesus Christ to all who believe. There is no difference, for all have sinned and fall short of the glory of God, and are justified freely by His grace through the redemption that came by Christ Jesus (Romans 3:22-24).
Is God the God of the Jews only? Is He not the

God of Gentiles too? Yes, of Gentiles too (Romans 3:29).

Therefore, the promise comes by faith, so that it may be by grace and may be guaranteed to all Abraham's offspring—not only to those who are of the law but also to those who are of the faith of Abraham (Romans 4:16).

If the gospel is for everyone, as we have seen, the Jews wanted no part of it. They rejected God's offer. At the end of his life, Paul made one final plea to the Jews. In Rome, he called together the leaders of the Jews. From morning until night he tried to convince them about Jesus. But when they refused to believe, Paul made this final statement:

The Holy Spirit spoke the truth to your fore-fathers when He said through Isaiah the prophet: "Go to this people and say, 'You will be ever hearing but never understanding; you will be ever seeing but never perceiving.' For this people's heart has become calloused; they hardly hear with their ears, and they have closed their eyes. Otherwise they might see with their eyes, hear with their ears, understand with their hearts and turn, and I would heal them." Therefore I

want you to know that God's salvation has been
sent to the Gentiles, and they will listen! (Acts
28:25-28).

In Romans 9–11, we see that this was all part of God's
plan to reach the Gentiles. If the Gentiles perceived that
the gospel was merely a Jewish gospel, they would have
never responded. So God bound Israel over to disobedience, so that the Gentiles could respond to His mercy.
"Israel has experienced a hardening in part until the full
number of the Gentiles has come in" (Romans 11:25). Historically, and even today we see that most Jews continue
to live in unbelief concerning the gospel of Christ Jesus.

Does this mean that God has rejected His people? By
no means! There is a remnant chosen by grace (Romans
11:5). In Israel today, there are many Jewish believers. We
were fortunate to have one such person, Yozi Ashkenozi,
as our tour guide when we traveled through Israel. Yozi
is a dear brother. Every time I think of him, I am
reminded of God's faithfulness to His people. No, God
has not rejected the Jew. He has promised that there will
be a day when all Israel will be saved. They will look to
Him whom they pierced and receive His mercy. All this
is God's glorious plan, predestined from the beginning.
As Paul said, "Oh, the depth of the riches of the wisdom
and knowledge of God!...For from Him and through
Him and to Him are all things. To Him be the glory forever! Amen" (Romans 11:33,36).

So what is God's purpose in predestination and election? It's that anyone who comes to Him, not by works,
but by faith, will be regarded as a child of promise. "As
the Scripture says, 'Anyone who trusts in Him will never
be put to shame.' For there is no difference between Jew

and Gentile—the same Lord is Lord of all and richly blesses all who call on Him, for, 'Everyone who calls on the name of the Lord will be saved'" (Romans 10:11-13).

Unity Between Jew and Gentile

Years ago God gave me a living example of the unity between Jew and Gentile in Ed Hecht. Ed is Jewish by birth, and he came to know his Messiah shortly after World War II.

I met Ed in 1972 when I came to Dallas to attend a citywide evangelistic campaign. Ed and I quickly became friends, and we have worked side by side in some capacity or another for almost 30 years. Never once in all those years have we seen each other as Jew or Gentile, but as close brothers in Christ. The unity between us is a spiritual bond. We are of one mind and spirit, united as God meant it to be among believers, both Jew and Gentile.

Most Christians have experienced such unity in different situations. It can happen when you travel to a foreign country and meet people whom you have never known before, and yet there is an instant bond of love. Somehow the unity of the Spirit bridges nationalities and all other differences. That instant rapport is the Holy Spirit in you responding to the Holy Spirit in them. There is no division in the Holy Spirit, only unity. Jesus is the answer to peace between enemy countries, as well as between individuals.

In Christ, all believers are one. Our identity is as Christians—not Messianic Christians, not white Christians, not black Christians, not Baptist Christians, not charismatic Christians.

> You are all sons of God through faith in Christ
> Jesus, for all of you who were baptized into
> Christ have clothed yourselves with Christ.
> There is neither Jew nor Greek, slave nor free,
> male nor female, for you are all one in Christ
> Jesus. If you belong to Christ, then you are
> Abraham's seed, and heirs according to the
> promise (Galatians 3:26-29).

In spite of this verse, many believers have divided themselves from their brothers and sisters in Christ by taking upon themselves man-made identities and divisive labels.

We have divided ourselves by denominational labels such as Baptist, Presbyterian, Catholic, or Pentecostal. One group unites around tongue-speaking, another majors in salvation through water immersion. One group thinks the correct day to worship is the seventh day, or the Sabbath. Other believers divide on their beliefs concerning the end times—you are either premillennial, postmillennial, or amillennial.

Then we have nationality labels: I am a Canadian Christian, an American Christian, a Chinese Christian. We even have racial identification: I'm a white Christian or a black Christian, a Native American Christian or a Jewish Christian.

In labeling, we separate ourselves and become a house divided. Our unity is broken with the true body of Christ. That is certainly not God's intent. We are all part of the human race and have been brought together through Christ and placed spiritually into one body— His body.

Any identity that we assume other than that of a child of God will steer us away from the rest of the body of Christ.

Just as some Christians foolishly become man-followers and start thinking of their Bible teacher or pastor as the one to be put on a pedestal, so, too, some believers allow their faith to subtly shift to sectarianism. Either direction is away from Christ.

Ask yourself: Does God want a Jewish church, a Gentile church, a men's church and a women's church, a white church and a black church, an American church and a Chinese church, a Generation X church, a baby boomer church—or does He want us to come together under one head, Jesus Christ?

In our fellowship in Dallas, we've seen God bring together people from every walk of life who are willing to be identified not by their skin color, ethnic origin, financial status, or denominational background, but by their faith in Christ. And do you know what the result is? Love!

At the time we started our church, I was involved in teaching Bible studies to executives. My background was as an executive, and it just seemed to make sense to minister to other executives. But one day God seemed to say, "Bob, when I walked the earth, did I have an executive ministry?"

"No, Lord," I replied.

"Did I have a high school or college ministry?"

"Uh, no, Lord. You didn't."

"What did I have?" He asked.

As I pondered silently, it was as if He continued speaking to my mind. "Bob, I simply proclaimed the truth about Myself, and the Father drew people to Me. Now you go do likewise."

As a result, when people ask me, "Does your church have a special ministry to minorities?" I reply, "No, I don't go out and try to reach any particular group or race or nationality. But in our church we have a greater mix of ethnic backgrounds than most churches that have tried to have special ministries targeting certain population groups." That's because as we lift Jesus up and proclaim His love, He draws people to Himself.

In the book of Acts, it's recorded that the Christians were "of one mind." So should we be. Instead, we divide into our little groups, not because we are of one mind, but because we flock together because of skin color, age, or marital status. The real and only reason for oneness is the common life of Christ we share.

The Lord's Supper: A Symbol of the Body of Christ

The oneness of the body of Christ is no better illustrated than in the Lord's Supper. God has given us this celebration to remind us that we're one in Christ with all other believers. Sadly, like so many other areas of the Christian life, the Lord's Supper has been observed in such a way that no one can see what it is meant to demonstrate. The way it is celebrated in most churches is a sad copy of a wonderful reality. It has become a solemn ritual instead of a celebration.

Let us look inside the typical church preparing for the Lord's Supper. First, the lights dim, the organ starts playing softly in the background. In most churches that I have attended, it sounds like they are getting ready for a funeral. Then the minister asks the people to look deep within themselves for any unconfessed sin. Everyone sits silently, desperately making sure that they don't forget some sin to confess.

At this point the minister opens his Bible solemnly and reads the verses from 1 Corinthians 10:27-32 about eating the bread or drinking the cup unworthily.

The people in the congregation get all introspective, thinking back on the week and the time they snapped at their spouse, or cut that guy off in traffic, or thought those lustful thoughts toward the new secretary. Or maybe it was the gossip about the neighbor lady that they listened to. Maybe it's the adult movie they went to see by mistake. And so now is the time to get truly remorseful and confess all these sins they've allowed to accumulate in their lives. Everyone wants to make sure they haven't missed a sin, so they don't eat or drink condemnation on themselves.

Then after a suitable amount of time, the pastor leads the congregation in the ceremony of drinking the grape juice and eating the bread.

While following this familiar ritual, how many people really comprehend the true meaning of the Lord's Supper? Don't the believers know that they are forgiven of *all* their sins—past, present, and future? Don't they know that everything was completed and finished for them at the cross?

Something is wrong, folks. In getting remorseful about past sins and asking God to forgive us, the finality of the cross has been drastically watered down and undermined. We have negated the cross, and we're living in unbelief.

How is the Lord's Supper, as it's observed in most churches today, any different from the practice of Old

Testament Jews who traveled annually to the temple to have their accumulated sins forgiven?

There *is* no difference. Once again, we've gone back to the old system of law and dragged it into the new covenant in which we stand. Combining law with grace is to nullify grace. Jesus could have stayed in heaven instead of becoming a sacrifice in our stead.

We have to come to a conclusion in our lives. Either our sins are forever forgiven, or we are still in our sins. Which is it?

It's no wonder so many believers walk around seeing themselves as "sinners." They are double-minded about their standing before God—especially when they visit church on Sunday and are reminded to "get right with God." As James 1:8 says, "A double-minded man [is] unstable in all he does," and this lack of understanding about the finality of the cross is spiritual instability.

Again, the problem is that we've mixed the Word of God with the traditions of men. Let us look at what the Bible really says about the Lord's Supper.

In 1 Corinthians 11:23,24, Paul begins with the familiar words, "For I received from the Lord what I also passed on to you: The Lord Jesus, on the night He was betrayed, took bread, and when he had given thanks, He broke it and said, 'This is my body, which is for you; do this in remembrance of Me.'"

By physically demonstrating a spiritual truth, Jesus communicated these words to give us a picture we could understand. After He broke the bread, He said, "This is My body, which is for you" (1 Corinthians 11:24). Christ, in dying for us, gave His body for us. The idea of a loaf representing the body of Christ is important. His body can't be represented by a bunch of crackers on a plate.

One loaf of bread is required to get the picture of Christ's body and what it means to believers who have lived since Christ walked the earth.

Two thousand years ago to see the body of Christ you would have to have been in Jerusalem and looked for Jesus of Nazareth. You would have seen the actual physical body of Christ.

Jesus, before His crucifixion, told His followers, "It is for your good that I am going away. Unless I go away, the Counselor will not come to you; but if I go, I will send him to you" (John 16:7).

What was He saying? The disciples didn't understand. Jesus wanted them to understand what was going to happen after He ascended to the Father. He assured them that when He went away, they would not be left on their own, but the Holy Spirit would come and live in them. He told them, "My body is going away, but I'm going to send My Spirit into you. And when I do, God will be living in you, and so you are going to be My body here on earth. So instead of this body which I am living in now being confined to one place at a time, My body will be throughout the world living in believers everywhere."

To give the disciples a visual aid, Jesus held up a loaf of bread, representing Himself, gave thanks, and broke it to show that His body would be broken for them. Then He distributed the bread to His disciples and said the immortal words, "Take and eat; this is My body" (Matthew 26:26).

Today, during communion, as each person takes a portion of the bread and eats it, what is it a picture of? It's a reminder of the day each individual came to Christ by faith and was added to the body of Christ. After everyone has eaten his piece of bread, where is the loaf? It is now in us. We are now the body of Christ—"Christ in you, the hope of glory." And even though many people who are separated by time, continents, language, age, and race come to Christ individually, they form one spiritual, invisible body, which is called a mystery: "Because there is one loaf, we, who are many, are one body, for we all partake of the one loaf" (1 Corinthians 10:17).

Do you see it? We have become the body of Christ here on earth. He is the head; we are His body. We are one in Him. When we observe the Lord's Supper, either in our fellowship in Dallas or in our conferences, I have people communicate this truth as they pass the bread: We belong to Christ and we belong to one another.

After the breaking of the bread, Jesus "took the cup, gave thanks and offered it to them, saying, 'Drink from it, all of you. This is My blood of the covenant, which is poured out for many for the forgiveness of sins'" (Matthew 26:27,28).

Look again at the last phrase. Why was the blood of Jesus shed on the cross? It was poured out for the forgiveness of sins. "Without the shedding of blood, there is no forgiveness" (Hebrews 9:22). His sacrifice secured our forgiveness forever. By trusting in Him, we become forgiven people. And yet each Sunday we hold our cup of grape juice or wine and mourn over sins that have been long forgiven and forgotten by God. We beg God to do what He's already done. Is that a response of faith? No, instead it's a mockery of the grace of God and the cross of Christ.

The cup of the *new* covenant means that we are totally forgiven, that we no longer need to go back to the temple or altar or church to offer up a sacrifice to God. In Hebrews 10:17,18 we read, "'Their sins and lawless acts I will remember no more.' And where these have been forgiven, there is no longer any sacrifice for sin." Jesus encouraged the partaking of the Lord's Supper to be in *remembrance* of Him. It was never intended to be an occasion to count our sins and name them one by one so we could gain new forgiveness. When Jesus died on the cross, He said, "It is finished." Will we ever believe it?

In 1 Corinthians 10:16, Paul refers to the cup as the "cup of thanksgiving." We are forgiven people. God remembers our sins no more. So, to the believer, the Lord's Supper should be a joyful time of thanking Jesus, remembering what He has done for us, and praising Him for His grace and mercy on us until He returns. What a joy it is that we can walk by faith in the truth that we are in Him and He is in us!

As we go about our daily lives, we are part of His body and ambassadors for His kingdom. What a marvelous privilege! "Now you are the body of Christ, and each one of you is a part of it" (1 Corinthians 12:27).

Jesus could not have given us a better picture of what He has accomplished for us freely. The Lord's Supper, when seen properly, shows the totality of God's grace in Christ Jesus.

I look forward to each time I can participate in the Lord's Supper. When its true meaning is celebrated while breaking off a portion of the bread and eating it with other believers present, I'm reminded of the Lord Jesus and His life we share as symbolized by the one loaf. It's a beautiful picture of God's plan of unification in love to make one body, or one new man, out of both

Jew and Gentile. It is a celebration of what Christ has done and the unity we share in Him.

But What Does All This Mean?

So what did God predestine? That both Jew and Gentile would be *one* in the body of Christ, united by love. In the traditional teaching of this doctrine of predestination, we've missed one of the most important lessons God wants us to know: the unity of the body of Christ. Understanding this unity affects the way we treat each other.

God's will is that all believers should manifest their unity by loving each other as Christ loves them, by accepting one another as Christ accepts them, and by forgiving one another as Christ has forgiven them. But how do we often respond to one another in the body of Christ?

Instead of unity and love, we see division and selfish ambition. Instead of acceptance and forgiveness, we see quarreling, backbiting, and evil of every kind. This wasn't God's intent when He predestined Jew and Gentile to be one in Christ. Paul explained God's intent for us in Ephesians 4:1-3: "I urge you to live a life worthy of the calling you have received. Be completely humble and gentle; be patient, bearing with one another in love. *Make every effort to keep the unity of the Spirit through the bond of peace*" (emphasis added).

The worthy life is a life that keeps the unity of the Spirit through the bond of peace. Notice, Paul says we are to keep the unity of the Spirit. We did not bring it about. God did. His predetermined plan unites us all in His Son, whether Jew or Gentile. When we recognize this truth and respond in faith, we will preserve what God has called into being.

If you have worn the Calvinist label or the Arminian label or some other identity, I urge you to let go of it and rejoice that you are a member of the body of Christ. When we grasp all that God has done for us, what other response of faith is there?

Faith's Response to God's Offer of Rest

GOD'S OFFER OF SALVATION is open to "whosoever will." Included in the package of salvation is His promise of a "Sabbath rest." The reason many Christians don't experience the rest God has in store for them is because of their unbelief. And yet this rest "remains" for the people of God (Hebrews 4:9).

This divine rest satisfies the deep longing in every Christian to know that God loves and accepts him or her unconditionally. God's earnest desire is for every believer to settle this firmly in total security. That's why the writer of the book of Hebrews urges his readers, then and now, "Be careful that none of you be found to have fallen short of [God's rest]" (Hebrews 4:1).

What does he mean? How can we fall short of something God has made ready for us? Verse 2 tells us, "For we also have heard the gospel preached to us, just as they did; but the message they heard was of no value to them, *because those who heard did not combine it with faith*" (emphasis added).

Every living person on this earth can read the Bible and know what it says. But God wants humanity to know what it *means*—in other words, He wants the Bible to be real and useful for everyday problems and situations. Unless it is accessed by faith, God's provision of rest is of no value. If we have a delicious meal placed before us, it won't do us much good if we just sit and look at it. We have to eat it to enjoy the taste of the food and to receive its benefits.

As chapter 3 of Hebrews closes, the writer says that the Old Testament people of God were promised a rest in the Promised Land, which was a foreshadowing of the spiritual rest we have in Christ. And he notes that they "were not able to enter, because of their unbelief" (Hebrews 3:19). The rest is there—it "remains accessible to every believer"—but "whosoever will" must "enter in" *by faith—by faith believing that in Christ we have everything, that Christ did it all, that we are hidden in Him. He finished for us every detail important to God, and there is nothing left for us to do but rest and trust.*

And just as the ancient Hebrews were to enter the Promised Land of rest by faith, so, too, the Christian's rest is accessible *only* if we cease from our works of trying to add to what God said was finished and live by the faith that pleases God—faith in the finished work of Christ. The writer confirms this by adding, "Now we who have *believed* enter that rest" (Hebrews 4:3, emphasis added). Are you resting, or are you still struggling to earn God's favor, forgiveness, and blessing?

Like salvation and every other promise of God, His rest is available to all, but is only experienced by those who will walk by faith. Rest is ceasing from trying to bring about what God has already provided. "Anyone who enters God's rest also rests from his own work, just as God did from His" (Hebrews 4:10).

In Genesis 2:2, we see that when God finished His work of Creation, "on the seventh day He rested from all His work." Why did God rest? It wasn't because He was tired. No, He rested because His work was complete, finished, and done.

Why does God want us to enter this rest? Because the work has been done by Him on our behalf and there is nothing left for us to do but enjoy God's benefits. Rest is a response to God's truth. It is a response of faith that pleases God.

To cease from self-effort and works is hard for most of us. We want to be involved, to be busy for God. We want to be well-thought-of by our pastor and our Christian friends. And yet, God differentiates between humanly motivated works and Spirit-led works:

> If any man builds on this foundation using gold, silver, costly stones, wood, hay or straw, his work will be shown for what it is, because the Day will bring it to light. It will be revealed with fire, and the fire will test the quality of each man's work (1 Corinthians 3:12,13).

As with salvation, it's God's way or no way. So it is with the provision of rest that is freely accessible by faith.

Four Results of True Rest

As a believer enters God's rest, there are several results or benefits. First, you're no longer trying to add to what Christ has accomplished on the cross. It means you stand firm in Christ's words, "It is finished." God is satisfied with the work of Christ on your behalf. The question is, "Are you?"

There are no more sacrifices to offer. There is no more pleading or begging for God to erase the black marks by your name, no more fear of punishment or guilt. There is just a heart that says thank you and rejoices in the truth that you are an unconditionally loved and accepted, forgiven person, with His life living in you.

The second result is that you no longer try to clean up your flesh through legalistic obedience. When God looks at you, if you are in Christ, He sees you covered by His righteousness. So instead of looking at yourself though man-made labels, you now can call yourself what God calls you, and *that* is your identity. You are a child of God, holy, righteous, complete, and perfect in Christ Jesus. What could make you more secure than knowing that the God of this universe is a Father who loves you and accepts you exactly the way you are? The faith that pleases God means resting in what *He* says about you and not listening to the world.

According to John 1:12, "All who received Him, to those who believed in His name, He gave the right to become children of God." In Christ, you are a child of God and you have His righteousness as your own. You can't make yourself more holy than He has already made you. You can't make yourself more obedient by trying to keep the law, but you can respond to the leading of the Holy Spirit who lives in you and will never leave you nor forsake you.

The Pharisees tried to live up to the law. What did it do for them? It made them proud, coldhearted, and merciless. It made them judgmental and void of any compassion. And it will do the same thing to us if we fall into the trap of legalism. That is what Paul was talking about when he listed his legalistic credentials in Philippians 3. He had been a rising star in the Pharisaical ranks, but in his heart he was a "blasphemer and a persecutor and a violent man" (1 Timothy 1:13). In this condition, Paul was shown mercy as he agreed with God concerning the condition of his heart and his deadness without Christ. He surrendered his intellect, his reputation, and all that he once thought was so important and traded it for the knowledge of Christ.

Paul came to realize that Christ *is* life, and all the achievements he strove for in the flesh were as "rubbish." The Pharisees were impressed with Paul and applauded his achievements, but God looked on his heart. Paul discovered that God was not impressed with the things he had accomplished in the flesh, or in the world's opinions of him. He was and is only impressed with His Son, Jesus Christ, and with the ones who walk by faith in Him. To those who do, He gives the right to become children of God. Obedience to the law can never bring this about. Only God's grace can elevate us to this lofty position of being called children of God.

The End of Ourselves

We find God's grace when we come to the end of our own efforts to impress God. Paul, before he came to know Christ, proudly boasted, "Look what I'm doing for You, God." But when his heart was humbled, he heard Jesus say, "Look what I did for you, Paul." As the Scripture declares, "God opposes the proud, but gives grace to the humble" (James 4:6).

Humility comes when we see our inability and become dependent on His ability. The Bible says that our hearts are wicked and deceitful. When we see ourselves the way God sees us, we can turn to Him and receive His very life and all that He has provided. Like Paul, we, too, must come to that same place and let go of all that religion says is important and rejoice in who we are in Christ alone.

We have to come to the end of ourselves—all of our efforts and trying. When we do, that is where we're going to find Jesus. I was counseling a young man one day who said to me, "Bob, I don't know what to do. I am disappointed with the world, with people, and with myself. I feel as if I am almost to the end of my rope. What should I do?" I replied, "Grease that sucker," because at the end of the rope is where you're going to find Jesus. Come to the end of your self-sufficiency, and you'll see that He is sufficient for all your needs.

Sometimes it is hard to let go. The world is filled with what I call "interceptors." It's constantly offering steps and aids to improve ourselves. It may come in the form of a pill that can make us feel better, a change of scenery, or learning to blame someone else for our problems. All these "helps" do is glue us to the rope and keep us dangling in self-sufficiency. They keep us from putting our total dependence on Him. But God's will for us is to let go of the rope and fall into the loving arms of Christ.

Many times we're afraid to go to God with our "little" prayers or requests. We only want to bother God with our "big" problems of life. Think about it. Can you imagine God thinking you had a big problem? We live our Christian life saying, "Lord, please give me a trip to heaven, but I'll carry my own load." But He says, "Cast your load upon Me for I care about you." The Christian life is a rest from self-effort—a rest into which we all are invited to enter.

The Bible says there's no righteousness attainable through obedience to the law, nor is there a rest for our souls that can be obtained through good works. There's not one thing that you or I can do to be righteous before God. There's not one action we can take that will gain us favor and entrance into God's rest. Given that, what should our attitude be? What is faith's response? How about believing God and *stop trying!*

God knows all of our needs even before we ask Him. He knows we have a need for righteousness before Him. He is the source of that righteousness through faith in Jesus Christ.

We want to be holy. We want to be loved and accepted. So God in His love for us sent His only Son to accomplish everything for us. All our deepest needs are met in our relationship with Jesus. When we look to our mates, family, or fellow humans to meet these needs, the results are disappointment and emptiness. These people are needy themselves, walking around with a void in their own souls. They cannot pass on to us what they do not have. Yet so often we continue to look to others in the hope of finding someone who will love and accept us unconditionally. So, we go from one relationship to another, from one marriage to another, frantically hoping to fill the emptiness inside. But the unconditional love we long for is a deep, spiritual need that can only be satisfied by Jesus.

Everything our heart longs for and all that we want to be, Christ has provided. In Him, we are complete!

Trusting God for the Past, Present, and Future

Third, trusting in Christ means living one day at a time, "forgetting what is behind and straining toward what is ahead" (Philippians 3:13). These were the words Paul spoke to people who worried and were anxious. Let go of the past. Give control of your future to God.

Friend, no one can change the past. It's over. It's gone. God promises us in Romans 8:28 that we can trust Him to cause it all to work together for good.

Stop torturing yourself over your past. What happened yesterday is history. You can't change it. The unkind words that came out of my mouth, I cannot take back. Believe me, there have been many times that I wished I could. Also, by thinking about what should have happened or what could have happened, we play the woulda-coulda-shoulda game long after the situation has passed.

Thinking and wondering about what the future will bring is not our territory, either. That, too, is God's country. Jesus told us, "Do not worry about tomorrow" (Matthew 6:34). Why shouldn't I worry about tomorrow? Because I can't know what it will bring, and thinking into the future is mere fantasizing. I don't even know if I am going to be alive tomorrow, and neither do you. God isn't involved in fantasy. He is only active in the *now* and in time of *need*. His grace is abundant and sustaining only for reality. I can only call upon the grace of God for what is happening to me right now, not for what I think is going to happen tomorrow, nor for what happened yesterday. He teaches us to see life from His perspective, not ours. We are new creations in Christ—the old has gone and the new has come (2 Corinthians 5:17).

Therefore, avoid counselors who charge you $100 an hour to dredge up your past. Instead, turn to *"the Counselor."* The Bible says to forget the past, but the world says to dredge it up, sift through it, and recall all the hurts, offenses, and abuses you have experienced. The only result of such a search is that you will find someone to blame for your misery and will thus procrastinate entering into God's rest.

Whom do you choose to believe: the Word of God or "hollow and deceptive philosophy, which depends on human tradition and the basic principles of this world rather than on Christ" (Colossians 2:8)?

Press ahead toward the goal of being in God's presence one day. Don't let your past be your master and the torturer of your mind. Give your personal history over to God and let Him renew it. Stop looking at life from your own perspective. Allow Him to renew your mind with truth so you can see everything and everyone through His eyes. Live one day at a time, trusting Jesus with your family situation, spouse and children, your occupation, and every detail of your life. So many people are deceived into thinking that they are a failure and have missed the boat, with no more opportunities for a redeemed future.

Thank God for Your Past...and Move On

An example of this is the true story of a woman I knew growing up. After many years, I returned to Indiana to attend a memorial service. While there, I received a phone call in my motel room at 5:30 in the morning.

The voice on the telephone belonged to Pat, a girl I hadn't seen since high school. She was utterly depressed and needed to use me as a sounding board. She had dated one of my best friends all through high school. At one point in their relationship, he had wanted to get married, but she thought they should wait until they finished college. As it turned out, in college he met and married someone else.

From 1952 to 1992 (40 years!), Pat had been living with the thought that if she had just agreed to marry my friend, how happy her life could have been. For all those years she had been in personal turmoil and confusion and ascribed it to this one big "mistake."

As she recalled the past, I told her, "Pat, you're living in a fantasy. If you don't believe me, go call your dream boat's wife, and she will tell you what you missed. I guarantee you will feel a lot differently. Who knows? His wife may be wishing she hadn't married him and is probably fantasizing how happy she would be if she had married someone else!" You can't call on God's grace for thoughts of fantasy.

God builds character into us through hardships, trials, and tribulations. So whatever your past is, thank God for it and *move on*. There's only one time you can feel something that is real and that's right now.

If you're in Christ, and Christ is your life, focus on Him. He will keep you in perfect peace. No one else can.

I don't need to examine Bob George's life. I know all about it. It's the story of a flawed man. All of us are flawed. Looking for perfection in each other is futile and destructive. Only God is perfect. Our flesh is rotten and unspiritual and will never make it to heaven, for "flesh and blood cannot inherit the kingdom of God" (1 Corinthians 15:50). But if you are in Christ, you know your inheritance and your destination: absent from the body and present with the Lord.

Christians who aren't resting in Christ continue to live in their fantasy about the future and the past. They continue to struggle with guilt and anxiety. But those who have entered His rest are learning to live one day at a time, trusting in Him to guard their hearts and minds in Christ Jesus. They realize that His view of life is much different from ours—that He is in control no matter how confusing everything appears.

Learning to see all things and people from God's perspective strengthens our attitude of trust, and we grow like a tree that has its roots deep in the ground. When the storms come and the wind blows, it will not be uprooted because it allowed its roots to go deep.

Are you living one day at a time, or are you still dwelling in the past? Are you resting in God's faithfulness today, or are you worried about what your tomorrow holds? There is only one way to experience the faith that pleases God. Let go of the past, quit worrying about the future, and trust the Lord for today.

Rejoicing in Our Weaknesses

There is one final result of entering into God's rest. And that result has to do with the way we deal with our many weaknesses. In 2 Corinthians 12:9,10, Paul, after pleading with God to remove his thorn in the flesh, received this answer: My grace is sufficient for you, for My power is made perfect in weakness. Therefore I will boast all the more gladly about my weaknesses, so that Christ's power may rest on me. That is why, for Christ's sake, I delight in weaknesses, in insults, in hardships, in persecutions, in difficulties. For when I am weak, then I am strong.

When I first read this, I was stunned. How could anyone *rejoice* in his weaknesses? Don't all of us have areas of our lives where we feel weak? Sometimes we even try to hide our weaknesses from other people, or secretly work to overcome them. But God says to recognize our weaknesses and be glad, because when we do, we will see God at work in us if we let go and trust Him. The weakness may never leave, but will always be there to remind us of our need for depending upon Christ. Jesus told us that without Him we can do how much? Nothing!

Are you aware of your weaknesses? Of course you are. And this is what frustrates so many Christians. We feel like we are the only ones who have these problems. We wrestle and struggle with our weaknesses, only to experience painful failures. It's sad that in Christianity people desperately try to hide their flaws, as if there is someone out there who has his life all together. There is only One who is perfect and His name is Jesus. Our focus on ourselves and on our failures takes our eyes off our perfect Redeemer and His finished work on the cross.

The Bible is full of real people with real flaws whom God loved. They didn't have it all together, but they lived by faith, trusting God to complete the work He began in them (Philippians 1:6).

We're all familiar with the weaknesses of Moses (anger), Abraham (fear of man), Sarah (unbelief), Samson (womanizing), David (fear, lust), and Peter (pride, fear of man), some of whom suffered an eventual downfall because they stopped trusting God and fell into unbelief.

In the New Testament, the apostle Paul, who was acutely aware of his own weaknesses, gave us the proper response when he said he would "boast" in his weaknesses (2 Corinthians 12:5,9).

Paul could boast because he knew a valuable secret about human weakness. He knew that his every weakness was simply an opportunity to see the strength of God at work in his life (2 Corinthians 12:9).

The bottom line is, if we are constantly trying to overcome our weaknesses through self-effort, then we can't at the same time rest in His strength and sufficiency. Our weaknesses are merely daily reminders of our need to depend on Christ. God knows they are there. In the midst of them, He has promised to complete the work He began in us.

Consider also that Paul knew from experience how to rejoice not only in his weaknesses, but also in adverse circumstances. For example, Paul rejoiced when he was in prison. This fact makes us take notice. Who in their right mind is happy about being in jail? But Paul knew that his joy wasn't dependent on circumstances or where he was, but on *who he was in Christ*. When our faith rests in Christ, He becomes our strength and joy in *any* circumstance.

Resting means leaving things in the hands of God, trusting Christ to work out everything for our good. And while you and I rejoice in our weaknesses and circumstances, waiting patiently for Him, we develop a thankful heart. "Be joyful always; pray continually; give thanks in all circumstances, for this is God's will for you in Christ Jesus" (1 Thessalonians 5:16).

Spiritual Las Vegas

Have you ever wondered how the city of Las Vegas came into existence? There really isn't any special reason for Las Vegas to be there.

However, a number of years ago a man from Los Angeles decided to put a gambling casino in the middle of the desert, in a place that contained nothing more than a gas station and a small grocery store. From those humble beginnings, and from the advantage of legal gambling in Nevada, Las Vegas has become a mecca for vacationers and fun-seekers.

But if you step back and look at the astronomical growth of Las Vegas, you quickly see the course of the human desire for more and more. The desire for gambling grew into a desire for entertainment. The desire for entertainment led to the desire for bigger and more spectacular forms of entertainment. Small hotels became big hotels, and big hotels became the ultimate in luxury.

They have built the flashiest, most exciting playground in America—as far as the world is concerned—right in the middle of the desert, in a place no one would previously have wanted to visit, let alone live in.

If your intention is to excite and gratify the flesh, Las Vegas is just about the most glamorous place you can imagine. Now having said that, I want you to know that I am not promoting a weekend in Las Vegas. I want to compare this phenomenon with the way many of us live our Christian lives.

We all know that when the Jews were freed from Egypt they roamed in the desert for 40 years. Sadly, much of Christianity has also settled for activity in the desert rather than the reality of a relationship that is found only in Jesus Christ.

All we have done in Christianity is dress up the desert to make it look as appealing as possible. We have built a spiritual Las Vegas, complete with big buildings, programs that cater to every need, entertainment, and anything that tickles the ear and makes us feel better about ourselves. In my early years as a Christian, the desert was my home, and I didn't know there was anything different to be experienced. All the glitter that once impressed me quickly became old as I became disillusioned and burned out by self-effort. I had substituted religious activity for Christ and missed His promise of rest.

But God never intended us to stay in the desert. His final destination for us is to enter His Sabbath rest. This rest is not a physical place, as was that of the ancient Hebrews, but an attitude whereby we rest from our works, just as He rested from His.

The generation of Israelites who escaped Egypt never reached their final destination. They refused to enter the Promised Land because of unbelief, so they died in the desert. They had the opportunity to go into the land and eat from trees they did not plant and drink from wells they did not dig. It was a land in which God had provided everything. But they never entered in. It was the next generation that Joshua led into the Promised Land. As the people crossed over the Jordan River by faith and reached God's intended destination only then were they able to enjoy all that God had provided.

The promise of this rest remains for us today. The writer of Hebrews urges us to "make every effort to enter that rest" (Hebrews 4:11). Have you entered the Sabbath rest—the promised land for the believer? You can do so by trusting in the complete and finished work of Christ through His death, burial, and ressurection from the dead. He has provided everything you need. Go in by faith and enjoy that which He has called you to. This is faith that pleases God.

Faith Expressing Itself Through Love

SEVERAL YEARS AGO I STARTED TO write a study guide on love. I thought it would be fairly easy, but I soon became frustrated because, as I was writing, it just wasn't falling together and flowing as I thought it should.

So I started reading through my Bible again. I said, "Lord, there's got to be a reason why I'm stumbling over this thing." As I reread Scripture, I found something I had never noticed before about love. I kept finding love being associated with faith and hope. It was a triplicate that was repeated several times:

> And now these three remain: faith, hope and love. But the greatest of these is love (1 Corinthians 13:13).

> For this reason, ever since I heard about your faith in the Lord Jesus and your love for all the saints, I have not stopped giving thanks for you, remembering you in my prayers. I keep asking

that the God of our Lord Jesus Christ, the glorious Father, may give you the Spirit of wisdom and revelation, so that you may know Him better. I pray also that the eyes of your heart may be enlightened in order that you may know the hope to which he has called you, the riches of His glorious inheritance in the saints, and His incomparably great power for us who believe (Ephesians 1:15-19).

We always thank God, the Father of our Lord Jesus Christ, when we pray for you, because we have heard of your faith in Christ Jesus and of the love you have for all the saints—the faith and love that spring from the hope that is stored up for you in heaven and that you have already heard about in the word of truth, the gospel that has come to you (Colossians 1:3-6).

We always thank God for all of you, mentioning you in our prayers. We continually remember before our God and Father your work produced by faith, you labor prompted by love, and your endurance inspired by hope in our Lord Jesus Christ (1 Thessalonians 1:2,3).

I realized it wasn't an accident that God arranged those words in that order. I also began to see that our desire to love one another is impossible apart from faith in Jesus, the Author of love. Faith in Jesus is rooted in the hope we have in Christ and is expressed through the love of God that can be passed on to other people. Since coming to see this, I've never taught on love in and of itself.

Love is the focus, the goal of faith that pleases God. This is much better expressed by Paul in Galatians 5:6:

"The only thing that counts is faith expressing itself through love." Paul confirms love as the aim and goal of the gospel in his first letter to Timothy: "The goal of this command is love, which comes from a pure heart and a good conscience and a sincere faith" (1 Timothy 1:5).

Faith, then, expressing itself through love for one another, is what pleases God.

Love is practical and never fails. And God has given each of us ways to express His love to other people as we live our daily lives.

When I was a new Christian, my heart was in evangelism, since the organization I worked for majored in evangelism. I was so excited about my new faith in Christ that I witnessed to everyone. I was shocked when some people said they weren't interested. How can you not be interested in eternal life? I started asking these people why. Here are some of the answers they gave: "You Christians are a bunch of phonies." "All I see in the church is hypocrisy. You talk about love, yet you can't get along with each other." "I don't see any reality." The reason they responded negatively to the gospel was the lack of love they saw among Christians. They didn't see the reality of God's love being lived out by those who claimed to know Him.

How did Jesus say the world would know we are His true disciples? He said, "All men will know that you are my disciples, if you love one another" (John 13:35). The world wants to know if Christ is truly making a difference in our lives. The only way they can see this is if we pass on to others the same love God has given to us.

After 30 years in ministry, I can recall having seen God's kind of love on a number of occasions. But more often,

I've noticed my own failure to allow faith to work through the love of God. Sadly, the more common example is of Christians wounding or even destroying other Christians and undermining what the gospel is all about.

Love Is the Best Example

One of the most powerful examples of faith expressing itself through love is the story of Dr. Joon Kim during the Korean War. Dr. Kim was a Christian pastor whose life turned into tragedy one day when some Communist terrorists invaded his village. The men forced Dr. Kim to watch as they killed his father, mother, wife, and all of his children except one. After the massacre, Dr. Kim was beaten and left for dead.

Later, the afternoon rains revived Dr. Kim. He staggered back to his home, where he found his youngest daughter whom the terrorists had overlooked. The two escaped to the nearby mountains where Dr. Kim then had to explain to his daughter why she would never see her loved ones again.

For the next several weeks, Dr. Kim was consumed with pain, anger, and bitterness over what had taken place, and he was angry at God who had allowed it to happen. Finally, in desperation, he cried out, "God, what do You want me to do?"

The answer led Dr. Kim back down to the village. He searched for and located the man who had led the raid that resulted in the extermination of his family.

He knocked on the man's door, and within a few seconds the killer opened the door holding a gun in his hand. Dr. Kim told the man, "Sir, I've come to tell you that I love you, and to tell you about my Jesus."

Dr. Kim's words penetrated the murderer's heart in such a powerful way that he surrendered his life to the Lord Jesus right then and there. For the next 20 years, those two men formed a partnership to tell others about Christ and worked together with one common goal. Many came to Christ as a result of those two men uniting, and because Dr. Kim was willing to be led by God instead of living the rest of his life in bitterness.

Hearing this story, I don't know about you, but where I come from, that kind of love can only come from God. It takes God's power of grace to forgive such unspeakable evil, and then to go to the man who killed your family and lead him to the Lord. In and of himself, no man can initiate that kind of love.

This supernatural kind of love is God's goal and is available for every one of us. Friend, if the world is going to see God's unconditional love, they're going to have to see it through you and me in our hardest trials. Our role is to yield our total body, mind, soul, and spirit to Him and allow Him to do His work through us.

This doesn't happen overnight, but only as we walk with Him in a trust relationship day by day. In our instant society we want everything right now, including spiritual growth. But God has His timing. He works slowly and lovingly as with a small child over the course of a lifetime, teaching us to trust Him more and more and to cast our dependency on Him only.

We see this same process in the natural world. For example, if someone wants to become a surgeon, he has to plan on at least eight years of medical school before he can operate or even write a prescription. If someone decides to be an attorney, he has to plan on finishing college and law school, and then must pass the bar exam before he can try his first case. All have to *learn*.

But in Christianity most of us are out working for God before we have learned of Him. We would not attempt surgery, cutting people open just because we took a first-aid course. And we would not step in and practice before the Supreme Court just because we've seen *Matlock* a few times on television.

God knows the folly in this. That's why He said that new believers shouldn't be given positions of authority in the church. They're not equipped yet. In God's eyes, there's nothing more important than getting to know Jesus and learning of Him *first*, before setting off to do things for God.

Do you remember the story of Mary and Martha as recorded in Luke 10:38-42? Mary was sitting at the feet of Jesus, learning of Him. Martha, on the other hand, was just plain mad. After all, she was busy doing all the work, while Mary sat there listening to Jesus instead of making herself useful.

That's exactly what is going on in the church today. It used to be an institution where a new believer could learn about and get to know God. In the book of Acts, when the church first started, the believers met daily for the apostles' teaching, fellowship, and prayer. But today people think it is more important to be involved in doing things. "Let's get busy for the Lord" is the prevailing theme. But the body of Christ is not an organization; rather, it is a living organism. We've substituted activity for Jesus and for the learning of truth.

If someone were to ask, "What is the Christian life and how do I live it?" what would your answer be? Is it being busy witnessing, reading the Bible more, praying more, doing more for God? Hopefully, you would answer, "None of the above." Instead, the Christian life is an abiding relationship with Christ.

Jesus told Martha, "You are worried and upset about many things, but only one thing is needed. Mary has chosen what is better, and it will not be taken away from her" (Luke 10:41,42).

Was Jesus being unkind to Martha by speaking those words? No, He loved her, just as He loved Mary. In fact, in John 11:5, Martha is the one of the two sisters mentioned by name: "Jesus loved Martha and her sister and Lazarus."

No doubt Martha loved Jesus, too. But her priorities were out of line, and she thought that the physical was more important than the spiritual. Business kept her from getting to know Christ better.

The same can happen to our lives. Most of the time we get preoccupied and put such importance on lesser things—things of this world—instead of focusing on where we are going to be eternally.

Let's turn our minds to the things that are eternal. Our citizenship isn't here, but in heaven. Therefore, Paul tells us in Colossians 3:1,2, "Since, then, you have been raised with Christ, set your hearts on things above, where Christ is seated at the right hand of God. Set your minds on things above, not on earthly things."

Even though we are still in the flesh, when we think on things above, we can make it our aim to love other people. Sometimes it's embarrassing to admit to ourselves that we cannot love. But that is exactly what God wants us to see. Without Him we have no valuable abilities. With Jesus, we can do all things. Remember, we can't pass on to other people what we don't possess ourselves.

Standing firm in God's unconditional love motivates us to pass this love on.

Most Christians know that the biblical standard for love is given in 1 Corinthians 13. But they mistakenly assume that hate is the opposite of love. In reality, it is *pride* that wars against love. For instance, love wants to serve; pride wants to be served. Love is patient; pride is impatient. Love is never envious; pride covets. Love isn't boastful; pride is arrogant and full of self. Love keeps no record of wrongs; pride has a mental filing cabinet where it stores every offense for possible future recall as ammunition. Whatever love is, pride is the opposite.

One area where this is apparent is in our attitude toward the perceived weaknesses of people who are not like us. Where love would overlook or resist stereotyping, pride wants to label others in neat categories.

Labeling Other People

One of the biggest hindrances to faith expressing itself through love is our tendency to label other people. Even though we admit that only God can know a man's heart, we observe others from outward appearances and immediately pull out our roll of labels and stick one on them. I realized this some time ago when I saw how our perception of other people will largely determine how we respond to them. I also discovered that we often base our perceptions of people on faulty or incomplete information, and thus we label them unfairly. It then becomes an obstacle to expressing love toward that person because we don't see him or her as a child of God, but as whatever his or her outward dress and behavior show us.

We form opinions of people by what they do, and then treat them accordingly. If a coworker snaps at you, you label her as short-tempered. If your boss corrects your work, you see him as critical and label him as a hard, judgmental person.

A wife may say, "I've lived with my husband long enough to know he's lazy." If this is the case, then all of her responses toward him will be clouded by the label of laziness. For example, if he wants to watch the last five minutes of the football game and she wants the garbage taken out, she'll chalk the delay up to his laziness. These labels and misperceptions concerning the way we see our spouses are particularly hard on marriages.

Men are basically nonconfrontational, even with one another. But if someone persists and keeps on pushing, either verbally or physically, some men will respond harshly.

Women often incite men to anger in their pursuit of wanting to resolve a problem that a man doesn't think exists. The result is that a confrontation is set afire. A man whose wife is in the habit of being critical and putting him down is likely to stand up to her one day, just to show that he's not a wimp. We want to be careful how we treat each other, always remembering to "do to others as you would have them do to you" (Luke 6:31). Neither spouse should be engaged in labeling or abusive name-calling, because hurtful words are hard to erase from memory.

We who are married, do we see each other as brothers and sisters in Christ? If you're a husband, your wife is your sister in Christ. She has weaknesses and strengths, pluses and minuses. Ladies, the same message applies to you: Your husband is your brother in Christ. As such, ask God to allow you to see your spouse through His eyes and not your own. When you do, God will give you a heart of mercy and compassion, instead of condemnation.

Our troubles start when we focus on the faults of other people but are blinded to our own shortcomings. Jesus said,

> Why do you look at the speck of sawdust in your brother's eye and pay no attention to the plank in your own eye? How can you say to your brother, "Let me take the speck out of your eye," when all the time there is a plank in your own eye? You hypocrite, first take the plank out of your own eye, and then you will see clearly to remove the speck from your brother's eye (Matthew 7:3-5).

This was brought home to me when I married my wife. Amy was from a different culture and had expectations of how her husband should show his love. I also had my expectations of how a wife is supposed to show her love for her husband. And guess what? Our expectations of each other were 180 degrees apart—and, of course, both of us were disappointed.

Not only were we failing to have our own expectations met, but also we had to suffer from the knowledge that our efforts weren't good enough to satisfy the one we cared for. I was convinced that any wife would be pleased with me as a husband if I just hugged her and was openly affectionate with her. I thought my way of showing love would be the right way for any wife. At the same time, Amy thought that any man would be happy with the way she expressed her love by doing things for her husband. But we were in for a surprise! Amy would say to me, "You don't love me. If you did, you would do something for me." And I would respond,

"You don't love me. If you did, you would be more affectionate with me."

It took a while, but Amy and I both learned the importance of letting the other person love us the way he or she knows best, rather than imposing our ideas on each other.

We also learned not to label one another even jokingly as "unloving" or "sloppy" or "inconsiderate." Instead, Amy and I look at each other as a child of God with the same need of being accepted by the other. God teaches us to see people the way He does. When He sees a man who is drunk, He doesn't see him as an alcoholic. He either sees him as someone who is lost and in need of life, or as a child of God who has a misplaced dependency, because he goes to the bottle instead of to God for peace. If we see someone who uses drugs, do we think of him as a lost drug addict, or as a child of God who was lured away by Satan into a lie of a misplaced dependency?

How many children have been deeply hurt because someone labeled them "stupid" or "ugly" or "uncoordinated"? When you name someone in a demeaning way, you're establishing a false identity in that person's mind, especially in children and young people.

We need to be reminded every day to think with God's mind and to stop identifying people by their weaknesses. All of us are flawed in some way. That is why we're told by God to love one another—warts and all.

Whose Approval?

Another hindrance is confusing approval with love. Some Christians think that having the approval of certain people (boss, spouse, parents, pastor) will bring happiness. In Galatians 1:10, Paul asks, "Am I now trying to win the approval of men, or of God? Or am I trying to please men? If I were still trying to please men, I would not be a servant of Christ."

The effort to gain the approval of other people is a never-ending cycle. It's a quick trip into bondage. We get so wishy-washy that every decision revolves around how we perceive the other person will react.

When I was first serving Jesus, that's what happened to me. Instead of standing rooted in Jesus' approval, I was seeking the recognition of the men whose opinions I respected. Many Christian workers are subject to this same bondage. But just as we can never please God through our good works, we really will never gain true acceptance or happiness through the opinions of other people.

After I came to understand my freedom in Christ and His total acceptance of me, the opinions of other people mattered less. I remember one time I was invited to a Dallas Cowboys game on a Sunday at the time we usually were at the evening church service. My friend had offered me his air-conditioned box seats with leather chairs and a television set to watch the instant replays. Without hesitation I accepted his offer. There are many who call themselves Christians who would be horrified that I, a Christian worker, would choose to go to a Cowboys game rather than attend Sunday night services.

However, I was going to the game. I knew the reality of God's Word: "Delight yourself in the LORD and he will give you the desires of your heart" (Psalm 37:4). I knew that I delighted in God, and I knew that He would give me the desires of my heart. And boy, did I desire to see a Cowboys game!

Did I feel guilty?

Not at all.

I went to the game, relaxed in my fancy box seat, popcorn in hand, waiting for the game to begin. Just then a man walked up to me and asked, "Are you Bob George?"

"Yes, I am," I replied.

"My name is Dan Majors," he said. "May I sit down for a minute?"

"Sure," I answered.

"I've been told that you know something about God."

"Yes, I do," I replied.

"Can we talk for a minute?"

Well, I never saw a single play of that game. We talked about the Lord the whole time and Dan Majors came to Christ as a result of that conversation. A few months later he invited me to his church to watch as he baptized his two sons whom he had led to the Lord. He's on our board of directors today. He is also my best friend.

The world would have said, "You need to be in church on Sunday." And a person who's led by his religious flesh probably would have felt better telling his friends that he chose to attend the church service rather than go to the game. But there's a difference between following tradition and following the Lord. God had a divine appointment for me at that game. And in having me meet Dan Majors, He gave me an even more pressing desire of my heart than watching a football game. Listen to the leading of the Holy Spirit, not the leading of men.

Paul says that you can't be a servant of Christ and still be trying to please men. Instead, when we have the faith that pleases God, we live our lives expressing that faith through love.

The goal to aim for is to abide and trust. Give up trying to do this or that, or trying to be or not to be. Instead, focus on the Giver, who is God, who provided the perfect Lamb slain before the foundation of the world—for us. If you're ever feeling sorry for yourself or think you're not worthy, just remember that Christ would have died for you if you had been the only living person in this world. That's how much He loves you.

When we give Him all we are, which is nothing, He gives us all He is—everything. That is called the exchanged life. He paid a debt He did not owe, for us who owed a debt we could not pay.

Faith in Christ changes everything. Christ releases you from all error, all bondage, and all false dependencies. And faith in Christ and in Him alone is the faith that pleases God the Father.

The Fate of Reverend Spurgeon

In the first chapter I mentioned Reverend Spurgeon, who pastored the popular church with the basketball court in the basement. A few years ago the parents of my childhood friend Tom Dailey came to Dallas for a visit. During our time together, I asked them if they knew whatever happened to Reverend Spurgeon. They told me that he was living quietly in a small Indiana town where he had left the ministry and gone into the paving business. They also told me that Reverend Spurgeon had become a heavy drinker and subsequently developed other problems. Also, they said that Reverend Spurgeon was terminally ill.

I was really sorry to hear this. That man had planted the seeds in my heart that years later germinated into a saving faith. I remembered how sincerely Reverend Spurgeon had ministered what he knew to us kids, and I felt a genuine debt to him, mixed with sympathy for his current illness. I wanted him to know that what he had done all those years was not in vain.

As I thought about this, I sensed God saying, "Bob, the way you feel about Reverend Spurgeon—that's the way I feel about him, too. Write him."

I asked Tom's parents for Reverend Spurgeon's address and wrote him a letter thanking him for the influence he had on my life during those formative years, for taking an interest in me, and for exposing me to God. I told him that those songs I sang in the church choir were still in my heart. Without sounding preachy, I explained that I had come to know Christ after so many years of only knowing *about* Him, and then I went on to explain the gospel message and how a man could know God personally.

I didn't hear back from him. But many months later, I received a letter from Mrs. Spurgeon. She apologized that, due to the severity of her husband's illness, he hadn't been able to write back. She went on to explain that her husband had recently passed away. She also told me that he had received my letter just two weeks before he died, and that when she would go into his bedroom at night, she would find him rereading my letter with tears streaming down his face. He read it over and over and over. As a result, he responded to the gospel message just as I had many years before when Dr. Bright shared with me. And then he died.

The desire to write Spurg (that's what we lovingly called him) wasn't something I mustered up. God placed that desire on my heart. When I received Mrs. Spurgeon's letter, I couldn't help but say, "Thank You, Lord."

Even though Reverend Spurgeon didn't know it at the time, God had used him to touch me in a special way. I was thankful that at the end of his life God could use me to touch him in a special way.

When we respond to God by faith and express our faith through love to other people, we really never know how God will use our life. For Dr. Kim, the result was a tremendous ministry with the man who had done him great harm. For me, it was the opportunity to bless a man who had been a blessing to me.

Such results are, of course, in God's hands. But my prayer is that you'll respond to God in faith, trust Him for the results, and rediscover the joy resulting from having the faith that pleases God.

In between the time that I started writing this book and its completion, my doctor notified me that I have prostate cancer. Due to the influence of an old college buddy, Jack Scheid, I went to take my first PSA test, a test for prostate cancer, back in 1996. Amy and I had met Jack and Connie in Dallas a few years prior to this and had renewed our friendship. I took a few additional tests over the next three years, and my PSA results were gradually increasing. My doctor strongly urged me to do a biopsy, which I reluctantly agreed to. After all, I felt like a million bucks, I had no symptoms of any kind, my prostate was the right size, and there was nothing to cause alarm except the high PSA results.

I went in for the biopsy, and back came the results. It's in these times when you really discover what you believe. My response to the news wasn't much different than had the doctor said to me, "Let's go have a Coke." My instant thoughts were "for me to live is Christ, for me to die is gain." There was absolutely no fear or anxiety, only the peace of God that passes all understanding.

For me to remain here on earth means I get to proclaim Him. For me to be absent from the body is to be present with Him. What is there to lose? The issue now becomes what to do in the meantime. Do I leave it alone and let it take its course, or do I look into alternative ways to solve the problem? My first thought was to give it some time and go the natural route. However, after thoroughly examining different treatments, I determined that the best thing to do is to go to a facility in Loma Linda, California, to be treated with proton radiation.

I'm anxious to get the problem taken care of and to get on with my life. This treatment has the least side effects of the several available options, and the results other patients have told me about are outstanding. As I considered my situation, I began to see how my physical condition was very similar to the spiritual condition of man. We don't feel dead spiritually. We have no outward symptoms, but the Word of God shines its X ray into our hearts, and we find out we're dead. Now the issue is, how do we get well? We then hear the voice of Christ saying, "Come to Me, all you who are weary and burdened, and I will give you rest." I had to take by faith what the Scripture revealed to me about my spiritual condition, just as I had to take by faith what the X ray revealed about my physical condition. That is what faith is—believing what has been revealed to you by God, and then acting on that faith by turning to the only One who can solve your problem: the Lord Jesus Christ. This and this alone is the faith that pleases God. I do not know what the future holds, but I do know who holds the future.

A Personal Invitation

If after reading *Faith That Pleases God* you realize you have never accepted God's offer of salvation in Jesus Christ—or if you simply are *not sure* whether or not you are in Christ—I invite you to receive Him right now. John 1:12 says, "to all who received Him, to those who believed in His name, He gave the right to become children of God." In Christ is total forgiveness of sins, total acceptance, and eternal life.

Salvation is a free gift that you accept by faith. You are not saved by prayer, but prayer can be a way of concretely expressing your faith in Christ. For example, here is a suggested prayer:

Lord Jesus, I need You. Thank You for dying for the forgiveness of my sins and for offering me Your righteousness and resurrected life. I now accept by faith Your gift of salvation. Through Your Holy Spirit, teach me about Your love and grace and about the new life that You have given me. Begin the work of making me into the person You want me to be. Amen.

Again, there is nothing magical about praying these words. God is looking at the heart that trusts fully in Him.

If you have received Jesus Christ through reading *Faith That Pleases God*, if your life has been impacted in other ways through the ministry of this book, or if you would like more information about our ministry, I would very much appreciate hearing from you. May God bless you with a deep personal understanding and experience of His matchless love and grace!

My mailing address is

Bob George
People to People
2300 Valley View Lane, Suite 200
Dallas, TX 75234

Other Books by
Bob George

Classic Christianity
Classic Christianity Study Guide
Complete in Christ
Growing in Grace with Study Guide
Victory Over Depression
Grace Stories

Additional Materials

Experiencing Victory over Depression
(Video and audiotape series)

The spiral into depression begins in our minds—our thoughts. Learn how to avoid the trap of self-pity and despair and experience the reality of Christ as your hope in the midst of *any* hopeless situation.

The New Covenant: Walking in the Fullness of God's Grace
(Videotapes)

Do you experience fear, guilt, and frustration in life? Certainly, this is *not* what walking in the fullness of God's grace means. In this series, you will learn how to let go of trying to earn God's acceptance and rest in what He has provided you through Jesus Christ.

How to Have a Proper Self-Image
(Four audiotapes)

If you do not have a proper self-image before the storms of life hit, you can drown in a sea of uncertainty. Discover the difference between a *good* self-image and a *proper* self-image, and understand fully who you are in Christ.

The Battle for Control
(Two audiotapes)

During the trials of life we are constantly torn between casting our cares on Jesus and trying to control circumstances ourselves. This battle is waged in every believer. In this insightful series, Bob George explains how you can overcome in this battle and live above your circumstances.

For more information, please write to:
Bob George
c/o People to People Ministries
2300 Valley View Lane, Suite 200
Dallas, TX 75234
or call 1-800-727-2828